AF539614

OUR BRANDYWINE

An Artist's View of His Brandywine Valley Home

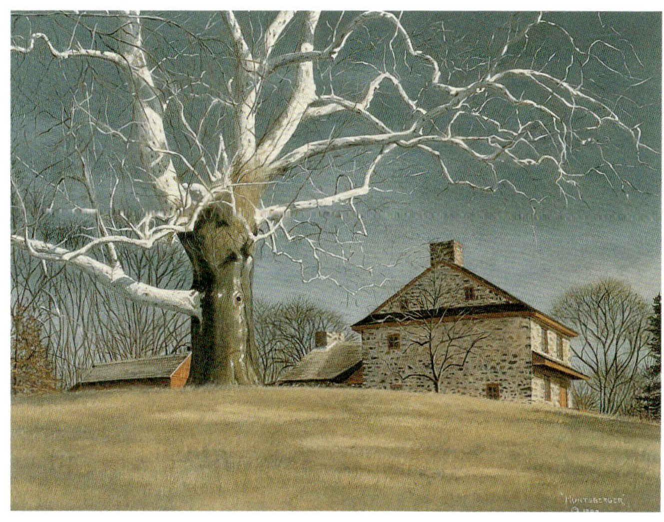

Paintings by James Robert Huntsberger
Text by Janet Davis Huntsberger

Cedar Tree Books, Ltd Wilmington, Delaware

Published by: CEDAR TREE BOOKS, LTD.

Any inquiries should be directed to:
Cedar Tree Books
9 Germay Drive
Wilmington, Delaware 19804
(302) 658-3994
books@ctpress.com
www.OurBrandywine.com

Library of Congress Cataloging-in-Publication Data
Huntsberger, James Robert.
Our Brandywine : an artist's view of his Brandywine Valley home / paintings by James Robert Huntsberger ; text by Janet Davis Huntsberger.
p. cm.
ISBN 1-892142-22-8
1. Huntsberger, James Robert. 2. Brandywine Creek Valley (Pa. and Del.)--In art. I. Huntsberger, Janet Davis. II. Title.

ND237.H92A4 2004
759.13--dc22

2004006116

Printed and Bound in Singapore by CS Graphics Pte. Ltd.

Contents

ACKLOWLEDGMENTS

First, we thank Elizabeth Y. Rump of the Chadds Ford Historical Society and Barbara E. Benson and Edward Chichirich of the Historical Society of Delaware, who served as guides to their societies' excellent collections. Thanks to Caroline Stuckert, Judi Lupi, John Ford, and Beth Rorke of Brandywine Battlefield Park who helped with the description of Battle of Brandywine and James H. Duff of the Brandywine Conservancy.

Thanks to textual editors and technical consultants Nan Stillians and Roberta N. Yarker Smith. Others edited specific sections of the manuscript: Susie Rogers of Hagley; Colvin Randall and Elizabeth Sullivan of Longwood Gardens; Kenneth Wesler of the Grand Opera House; Suzanne Smith of Marian Coffin Garden at Gibraltar; and Mrs. Sylvester De Paulo of Maplebrook Farm.

Tika Day shared her historical research about Jessop's Tavern and information concerning the schooner that sits in the tavern's front window.

Charles F. Hummel spotted popular local myths embedded in my prose—fables passing for fact elsewhere—now exorcised from descriptions here. Many made helpful suggestions and comments: Mrs. David Craven, U.S. Senator Thomas R. Carper, Barbara Dougherty, Patricia Durchholz, Julia M. McCabe, Barbara Moore, and Jane Stalzer.

Finally, we thank all those patrons who have chosen Huntsberger art for their homes and offices and who suggested this bound collection. They helped to make it possible.

Introduction

Originally this was a valley inhabited by people of the Lenni-Lenape nation. Today the valley of the Brandywine River, or creek as it is known locally, retains most of its pristine beauty because many latter-day inhabitants work diligently to keep it unspoiled. Luckily the fast-moving stream powered the early industrialization of the Brandywine because burning wood or coal could have polluted the entire valley.

Many farsighted people actively planned land use. With four notable exceptions, they are too numerous to mention. Early industrialist William P. Bancroft (1835-1928) donated land for parks along the Creek within the city of Wilmington. Pierre S. du Pont (1870-1954) purchased Peirce's Park to save its historic tree collection from timber cutters and built his world-renowned Longwood Gardens. Henry Francis du Pont (1880-1969) provided a green oasis on the East Coast by making the one thousand acres of Winterthur available to the public. He arranged for additional Winterthur land to be available for compatible use. George A. "Frolic" Weymouth (1935-) formed the Brandywine Conservancy in 1967 to retain the open character of hundreds of Pennsylvania acres and to save them from industrialization. These men were farsighted stewards of the environment who worked to beautify and protect the land that was home to the Lenni-Lenape nation.

The Brandywine Valley is home to entrepreneurs and industrialists. The early mill owners on the Brandywine Creek formed a cooperative to maintain the high quality of the Brandywine brand flour they sold. They risked British destruction of their mills to supply flour to George Washington's army. After the Revolutionary War the du Pont family came to Wilmington, Delaware. They sold the first black powder from their Brandywine mills in 1804. Their small venture grew into the chemical giant E. I. du Pont de Nemours and Company.

The Brandywine Valley is home to artists. Howard Pyle is called the Father of American Illustration. He taught many distinguished artists including N. C. Wyeth, whose son Andrew and grandson James still paint here. Today countless other very accomplished artists live and work in the Brandywine Valley.

This book is an affectionate tour of our home—the Brandywine Valley—as interpreted by oil paintings and italicized comments that reflect the artist's viewpoint. It is not a definitive history of the region, its people, industry, politics, or art. It is a guide for visitors to our beautiful historic and educational locations. We include an annotated bibliography with suggestions for further reading because we hope you will want to learn more about our Brandywine Valley.

Janet Davis Huntsberger

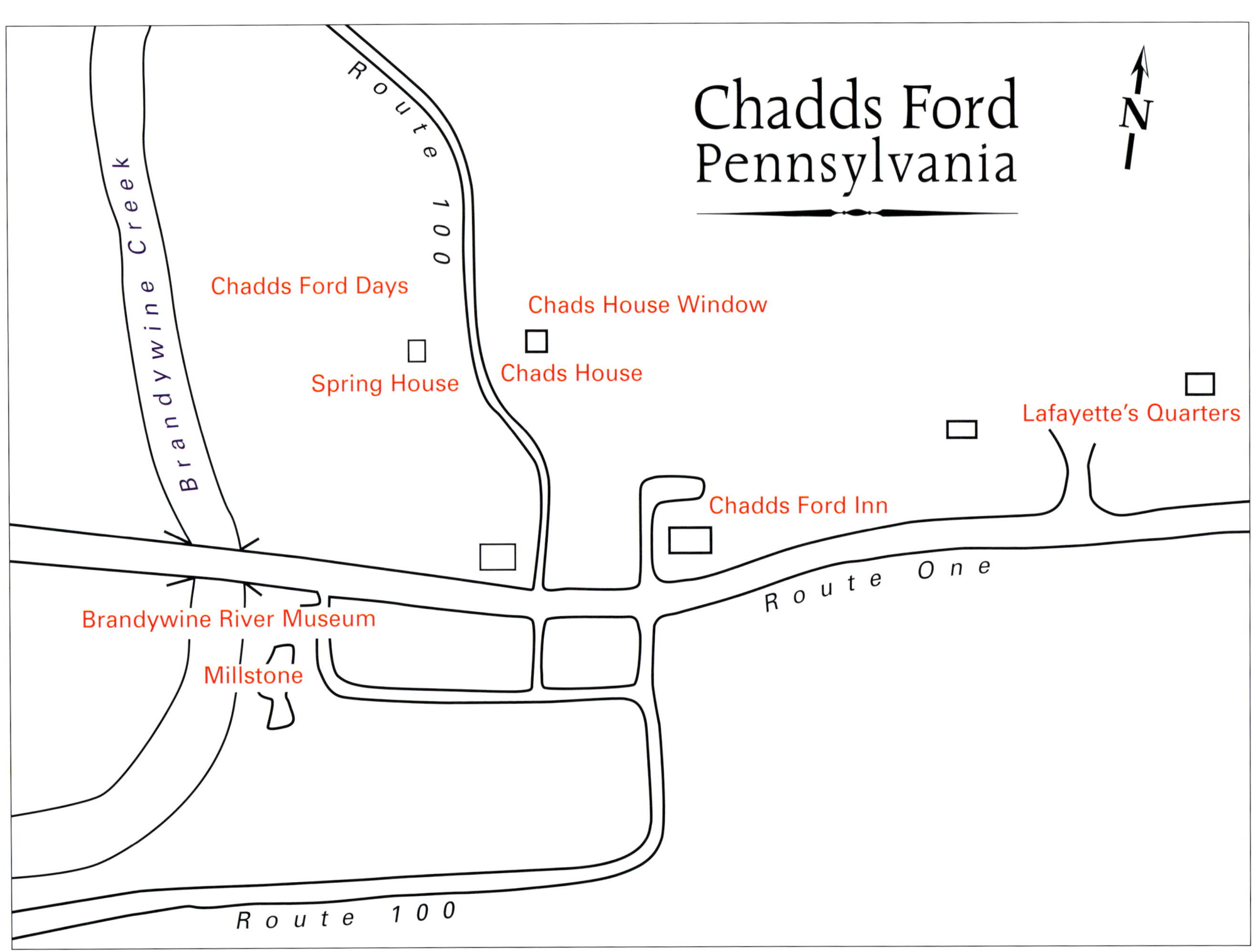
Chadds Ford
Pennsylvania
N
Route 100
Brandywine Creek
Chadds Ford Days
Chads House Window
Spring House
Chads House
Lafayette's Quarters
Chadds Ford Inn
Route One
Brandywine River Museum
Millstone
Route 100

Chapter One

Chadds Ford, Pennsylvania

The village of Chadds Ford, which surrounds the intersection of Routes 1 and 100 near the Brandywine River, was named for John Chads who operated a ferry across the shallow ford that bears his name. The Chads family is known variously as Chad, Chadsey, and Chadd.

For such a small town Chadds Ford offers an unusual number of interesting sites and activities. The home John Chads built years ago on Route 100 about one-half mile north of Route 1 is open to the public. The Brandywine Battlefield Park has well-maintained buildings from the 1777 period. Its hills are so steep one marvels that Revolutionary War troops were able to fight after climbing them. The Brandywine River Museum has peerless collections of paintings by Wyeth family members, Howard Pyle, and other American illustrators. The Chadds Ford Inn is a fine restaurant with a historic past.

In April the parents of Chadds Ford Elementary School students host an excellent art show featuring dozens of local artists. In September Chadds Ford Days are held. In December the Chadds Ford Gallery hangs miniature original works by local artists for eager patrons to choose as holiday gifts.

John Chads House

In 1725 John Chads built this charming house with two corner fireplaces and recessed storage niches framed into the woodwork above the mantels. With storage room at a premium, it was natural to use the space adjoining the chimney flues of corner fireplaces to keep household items.

The attic contains the original roof rafters and collar beams, which were built on the ground and then, with much effort, raised into position. Each beam has a carved Roman numeral used to place the wooden-pegged roof sections into proper location.

The widowed Mrs. Chads lived in the house during the Revolutionary War. Although her home was in the direct line of British cannon and musket fire during the Battle of Brandywine, she refused to leave it.

Over the years the house fell into disrepair, but since the Chadds Ford Historical Society purchased it in 1968, it has been fully restored. The house opened to the public in 1972. Much of the original oak flooring, woodwork, and hardware are still in the house. When the plaster was removed during the restoration, the original room partitions, made of feather-edged poplar, were discovered.

I have always been fascinated by Pennsylvania's colonial stone houses. This one has a special meaning for me.

24" x 30" Oil on Canvas 1993 Corporate Collection

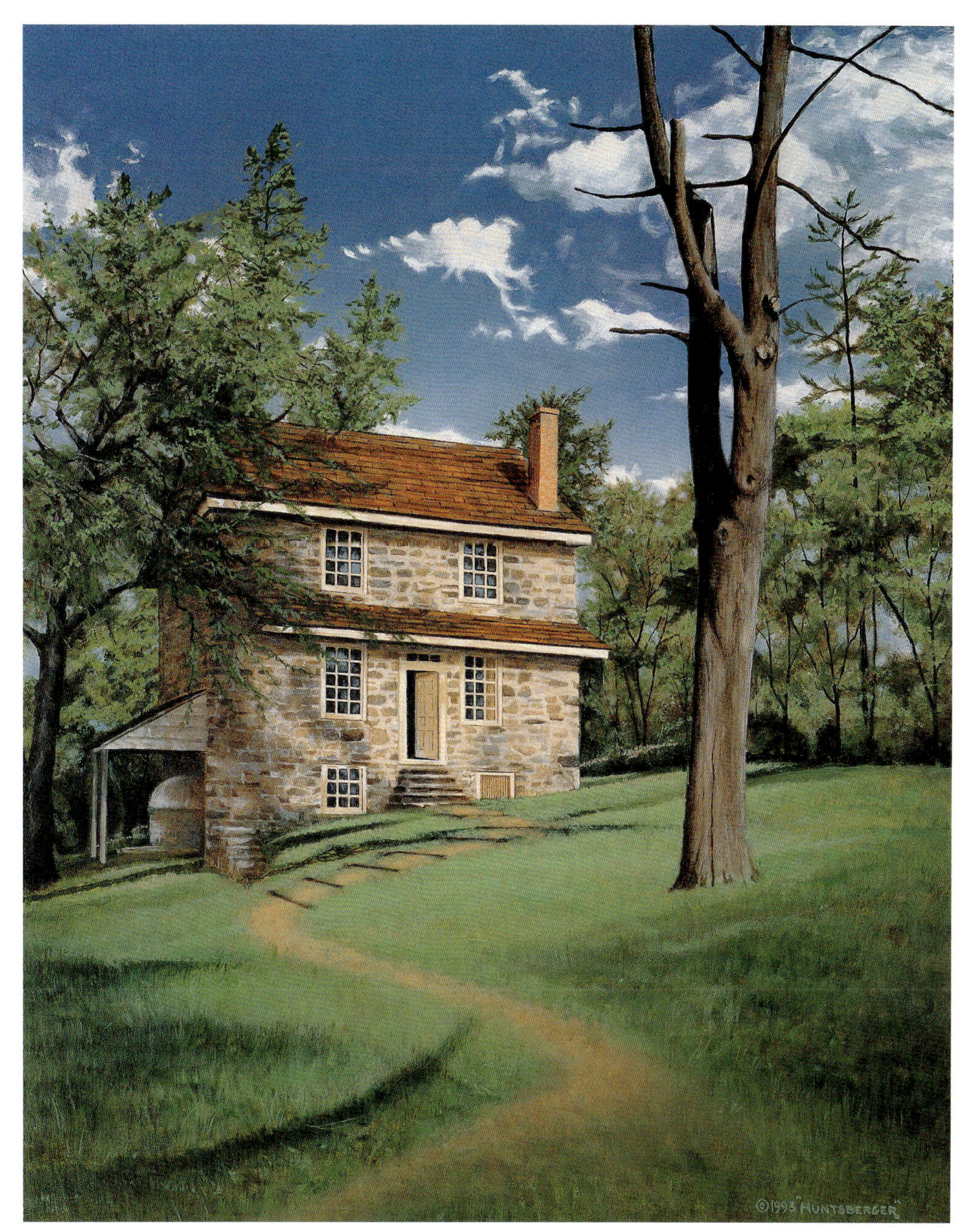
©1993 "HUNTSBERGER"

Chads House Window

This window is in the basement kitchen of the John Chads House. Its wide sill and imperfect glass lend charm to this interesting room.

The kitchen is paved with unusually large flat stone slabs and has a spacious cooking fireplace with a double lintel tapered downward on both the front and back.

A big beehive oven projects into the yard. The oven is in regular use on summer weekends and during special tours, when visitors may observe the baking process and, at the end of the day, purchase the fresh bread.

During a visit to the Chads House kitchen, I found the play of light and the distortion of the outdoor scene by the old glass to be ideal for a painting. I took some reference photos, painted the oil in my studio, and kept the painting for our own collection.

16" x 20" Oil on canvas 1993 Collection of Janet & JR Huntsberger

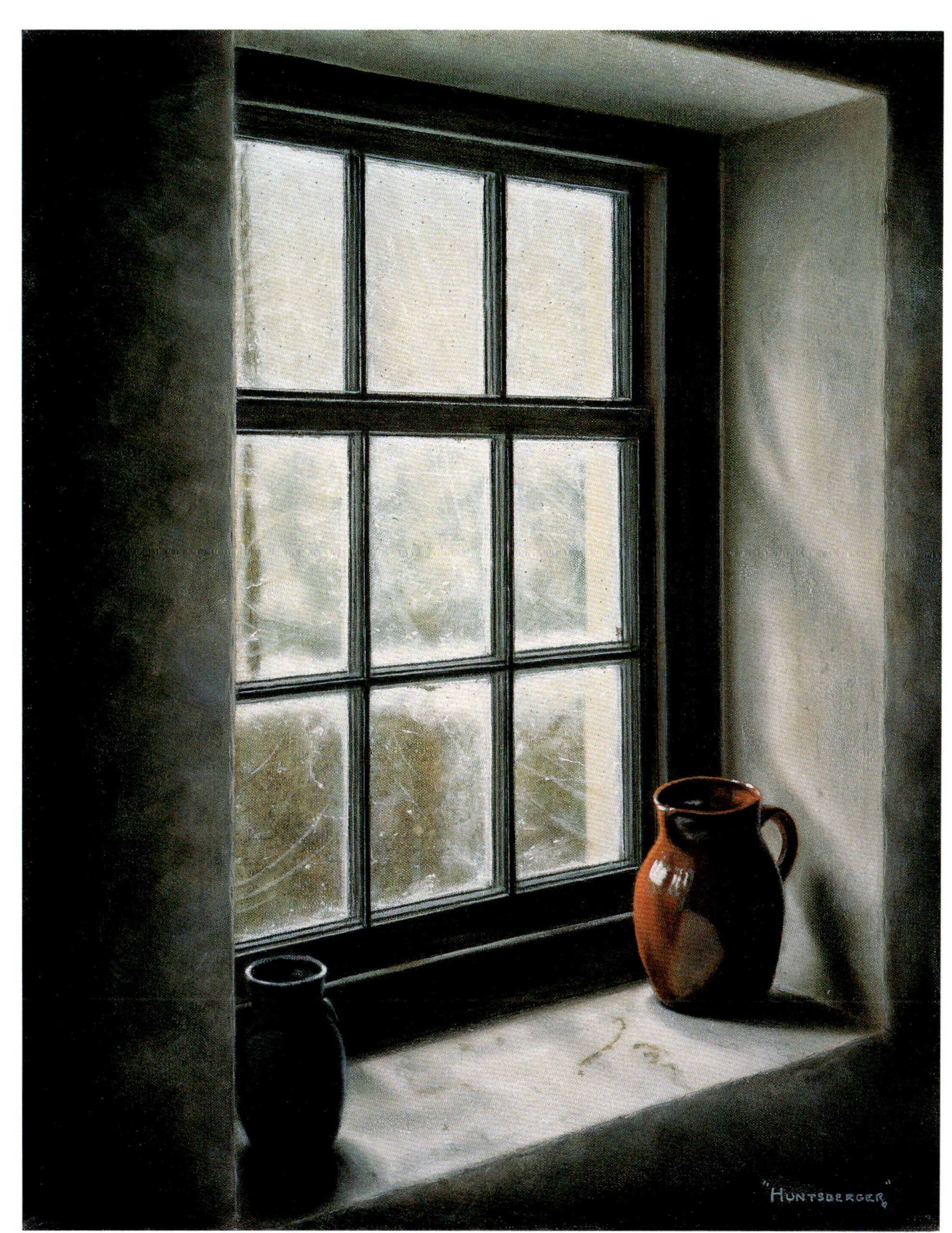
"HUNTSBERGER"

Springhouse

Across the road from the John Chads House is its completely restored springhouse, located under trees to shade it from direct sunlight during the summer. Tenants originally used the spacious first floor, which has a corner fireplace and a loft. During the nineteenth century the first floor was a schoolhouse.

The floor of the spring level is a stone platform around which water flows. Most foods were cooled by placing them directly into the spring. Shelves and niches, approximately four feet above the water, were used to cool foods that could not be put into water.

The walls are one-and-one-half-feet thick and made of fieldstone instead of more expensive brick. Whitewashing the walls gave the springhouse a finished appearance.

During the Battle of Brandywine the British fired cannons over the creek at Washington's troops stationed on high ground behind the John Chads House. Patchwork in the masonry suggests that a British cannonball may have damaged the springhouse.

During the annual Chadds Ford Days celebration our art display is near the springhouse. On especially hot days we can find cool respite there.

28" x 22" Oil on canvas 1993 Corporate Collection

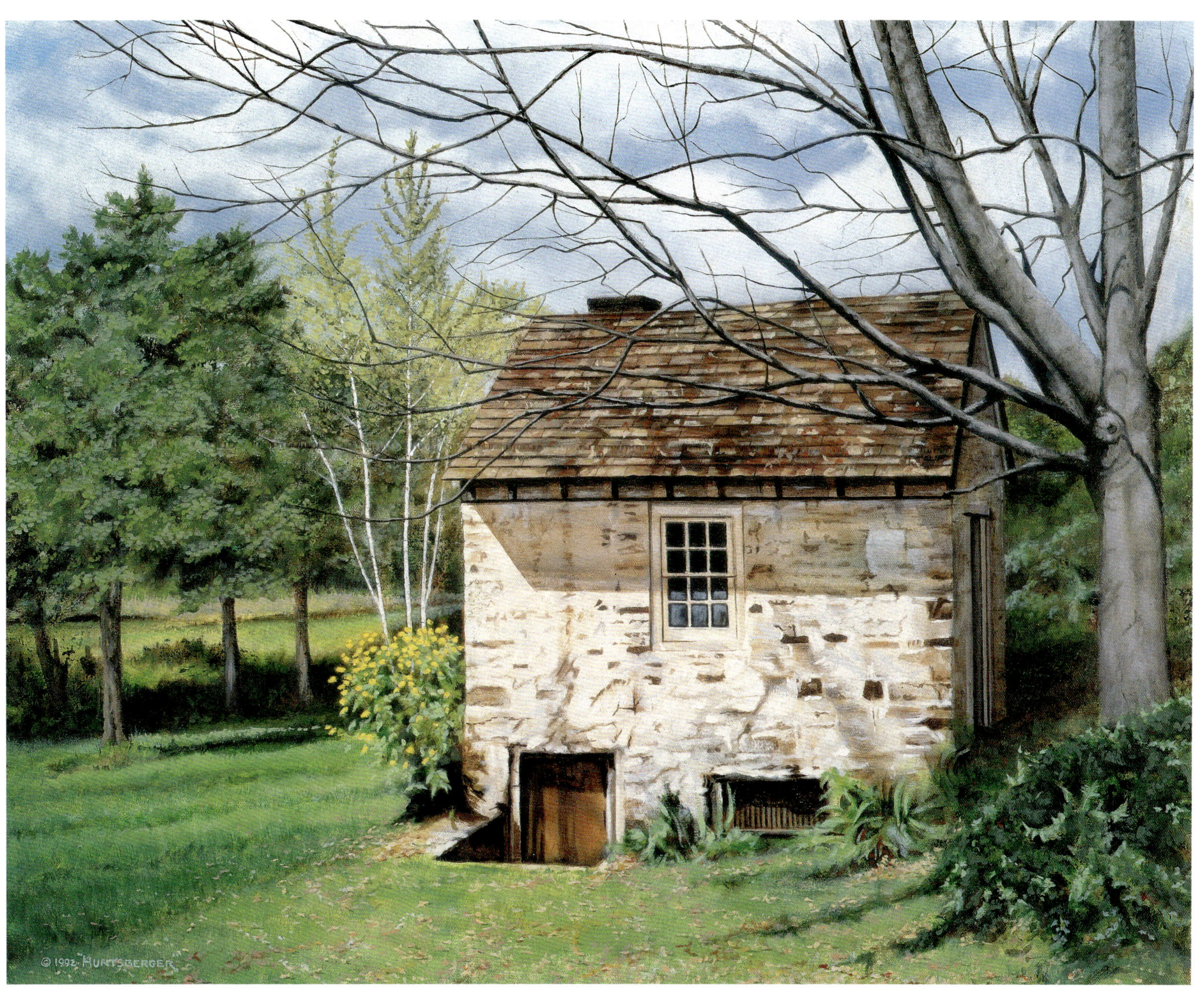
© 1992 HUNTSBERGER

Lafayette's Quarters

On September 11, 1777, the Revolutionary War Battle of Brandywine was fought on ten square miles of fields and hills surrounding Chadds Ford. The British were marching northeast from the Chesapeake Bay to Philadelphia to capture the colonial capitol city.

The main road to Philadelphia crossed the Brandywine River at Mr. Chads's ford. Because General Washington was convinced that the British, commanded by Lord Howe, would concentrate their attack there, he placed his troops on the east bank of the Brandywine to secure the fords nearest the main road. But Howe split his forces, sending part to Chads's ford and sending the majority twelve miles north to cross the Brandywine at unguarded fords. After crossing the river, the British marched south to outflank the right wing of the Americans near Birmingham Meeting House. The noise coming from the Birmingham conflict signaled the British troops posted on the road to Philadelphia to rush Mr. Chads's ford.

Superior tactics, greater troop strength, and better use of the local terrain allowed Howe to defeat Washington; however, the outnumbered Americans earned grudging respect from the British for fighting them on their own terms and living to fight again. In mid-December the Americans settled at Valley Forge— where they spent the winter, cold, poorly fed, and ill-sheltered—while the British moved to the warmth, comfort, and plenty of Philadelphia.

On the eve of the battle the Marquis de Lafayette, a young French volunteer aide to General Washington, was quartered in the home of Gideon Gilpin, a prosperous Quaker farmer. Although Lafayette had extensive military training his first actual combat experience was the Battle of Brandywine.

Lafayette's Quarters appears today much as it did in 1777, although later additions were attached to the original 1745 stone dwelling. It is part of the Brandywine Battlefield Park, administered by the Pennsylvania Historical and Museum Commission.

The carefully tended 368-year-old sycamore tree still stands as one of our most recognizable Brandywine Valley landmarks.

While studying at Bethany College, long before coming to the Brandywine Valley, I admired Andrew Wyeth's beautiful pencil study of this tree. I didn't know the tree was a sycamore or where it grew. When I visited the battlefield, I recognized Wyeth's tree. I searched for a vantage point for a nice composition and used a polarized filter for my reference photos. The filter darkened the clear winter sky to create the scene I wanted to paint.

24" x 18" Oil on canvas 1988 Corporate Collection

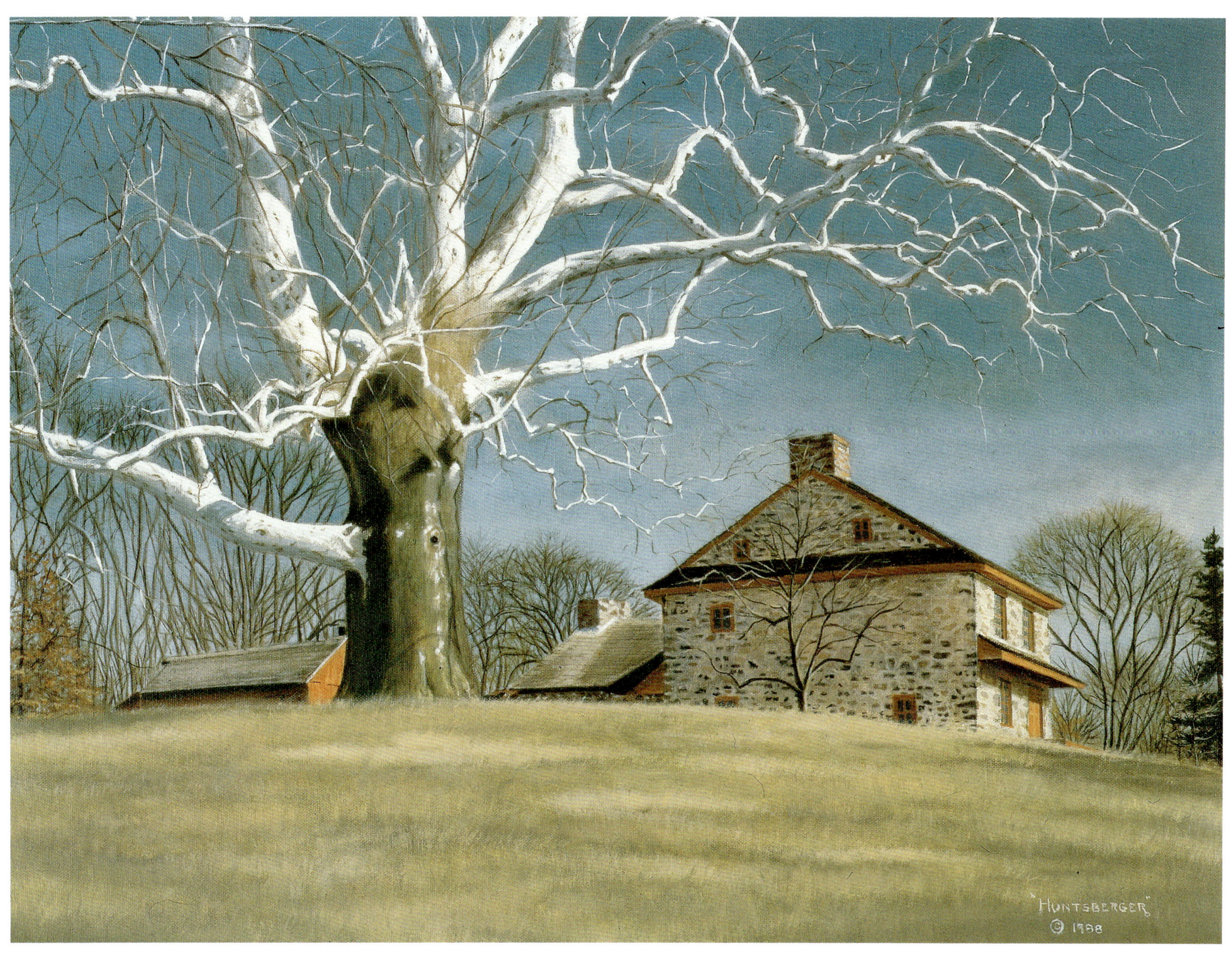
"HUNTSBERGER"
© 1988

Chadds Ford Days

Each September on the first weekend after Labor Day, the people of Chadds Ford commemorate the 1777 Battle of Brandywine and celebrate the village's past.

Chadds Ford Days are held in the meadow near the John Chads springhouse across the road from the John Chads House on Route 100 just north of Route 1. The celebration offers colonial crafts, local art, pony and hay rides, children's activities, music, and excellent food. (Don't miss the apple cider donuts early in the morning!) A bagpiper wanders through the meadow and plays during breaks in the scheduled musical program.

Craftsmen demonstrate colonial era crafts and sell their wares. One can observe the carding, spinning, and weaving that turns wool into fabric or watch a blacksmith shape iron on his anvil. Local artists display and sell their paintings near the Chads's springhouse.

Many festival volunteers dress in Revolutionary War period costumes. "George Washington" and "Benjamin Franklin" tour the meadow to discuss eighteenth-century events with visitors.

Volunteers demonstrate cooking and baking in the kitchen of the Chads House. Fresh bread, jams, and jellies are sold near the springhouse. Native perennial flower plants are also available.

Chadds Ford Days fosters a sense of community among local residents and the event provides funds to preserve and staff the Chadds Ford Historical Society's eighteenth-century buildings.

I composed this scene from several reference photos.
The most difficult part was inverting the light and shadows on the colonial soldiers to be consistent with the light in the rest of the painting.

28" x 22" Oil on canvas 1990 Corporate Collection

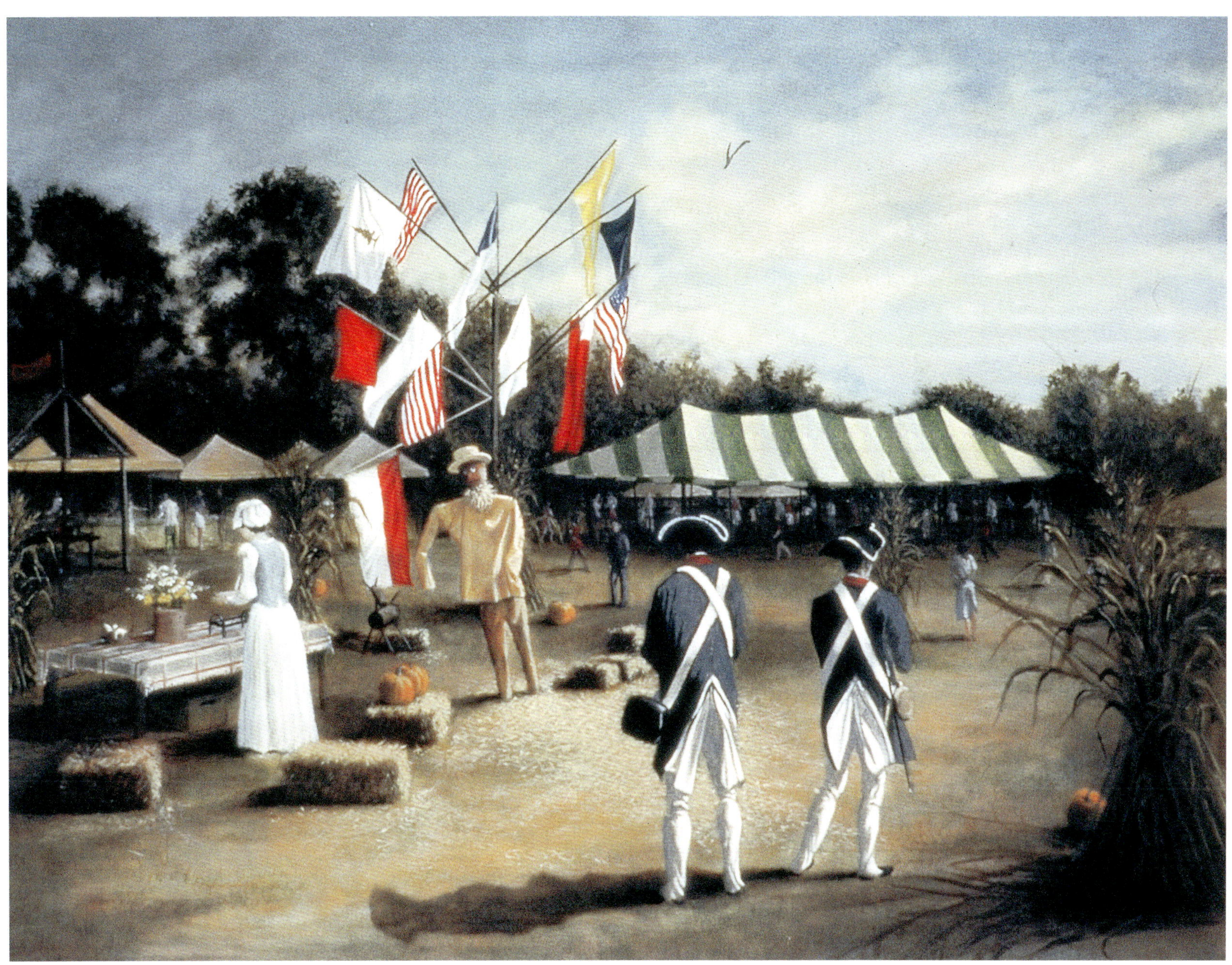

Chadds Ford Inn

In 1736 John Chads received permission from the courts of Chester County to open a public inn close to his Brandywine ferry. An eighteenth-century traveler wrote of Chads's Tavern:

"It is a house that lies most convenient to the ford or ferry boat on the Brandywine and keeps the best entertainment for man and horse on the upper road from Maryland to Philadelphia and likewise keeps a very orderly house, not allowing either drunkenness or swearing."

Both the tavern and the ferry were profitable businesses. When travelers were detained by icy weather, they stayed at the inn until the weather improved. When John Chads died in 1760, he left the inn to his nephew, Joseph Davis, who moved the tavern to this spacious building.

In September 1777 Joseph Davis, as proprietor of the tavern, entertained American officers before the Battle of Brandywine. As a result he suffered at the hands of the British. After the American loss, the British vandalized the inn. They drained liquor, confiscated supplies, burned furniture, and smashed mirrors. Old tax records reveal the extent of Davis's losses.

During the twentieth century the Theodore family owned and carefully preserved the building. They managed a first-class restaurant, maintained the inn's colonial character, and displayed their impressive collection of Wyeth paintings. In later years, beautifully framed copies of their paintings were substituted to protect the originals. The upstairs sleeping rooms for eighteenth-century storm-bound travelers were transformed into private dining rooms.

Today the Chadds Ford Inn operates much as it did in earlier days. The dining rooms are painted in neutral tones and adorned with memorable local art. The aroma of excellent cuisine and warm popovers wafts throughout.

For more than forty years the Chadds Ford Inn has been one of my favorite restaurants, as well as a historic building. I believed it to be a deserving subject for a painting.

24" x 18" Oil on canvas 1997 Private Collection

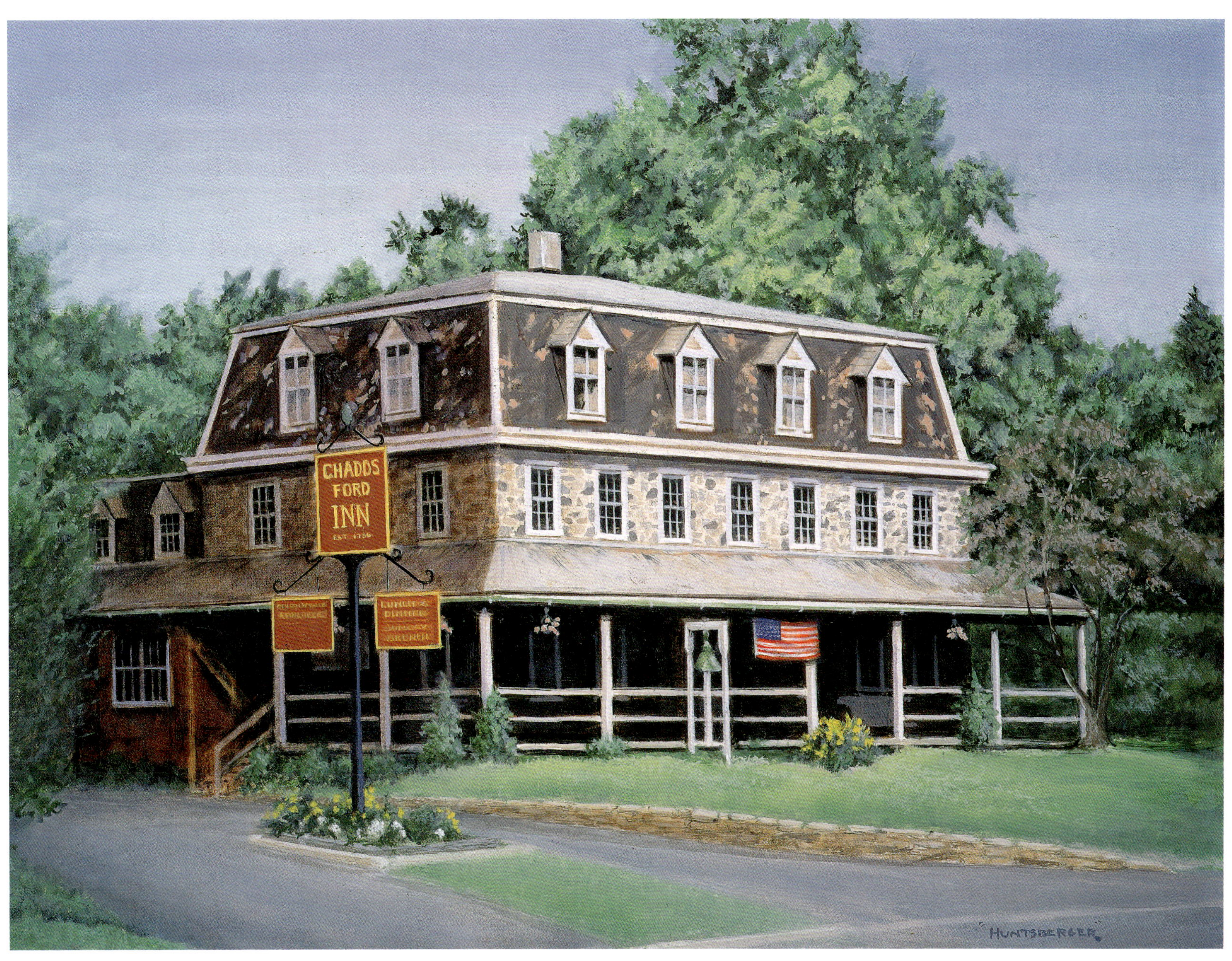
CHADDS
FORD
INN
HUNTSBERGER

Brandywine River Museum

The Brandywine Conservancy, formed in 1967 under the leadership of George "Frolic" Weymouth, protects the artistic, natural, and historical resources of the Brandywine region and shares them with natives and visitors from around the world. One of its first conservation projects was saving Hoffman's Mill, now the main section of the Brandywine River Museum in Chadds Ford.

This commonplace 1864 gristmill was stabilized and refurbished to provide gallery space for a remarkable art collection. The original hand-hewn beams, supporting posts, and wide plank flooring were reinforced and retained. A huge, soaring, contemporary glass tower, added to provide light-filled lobbies on each level, provides sweeping views of the quiet, unspoiled Brandywine Creek. Remarkable attention to detail blends the very old mill portion with the contemporary addition. For example, brick-floored elevators echo the brick-floored lobby, and enclosed curved stairwells echo the glass tower.

The Brandywine River Museum is internationally known for its incomparable collections of Wyeth paintings, American illustrations, landscape, and still life paintings. Most of this art was influenced by Howard Pyle, known as the Father of American Illustration, who taught art in Chadds Ford and Wilmington, Delaware. N. C. Wyeth and Frank Schoonover were two of his students. Pyle fostered the Brandywine tradition of enhancing reality with emotional and personal interpretation.

Outside, gardens of native wildflowers disguise the parking lots, providing glorious color from spring through autumn. A walking trail meanders from the museum along the Brandywine under the traffic-laden Route 1 bridge through a wetland (on an elevated boardwalk) to the meadow adjoining the John Chads House.

I had visited the mill before it was reconstructed to become the Brandywine River Museum. As a member of the Brandywine Conservancy, I visit frequently and have long thought I would like to paint an oil but did not find an aspect that satisfied me until I saw this scene with the strong backlight.

8" x 10" Oil on board 2001 Collection of Regina M. Landis

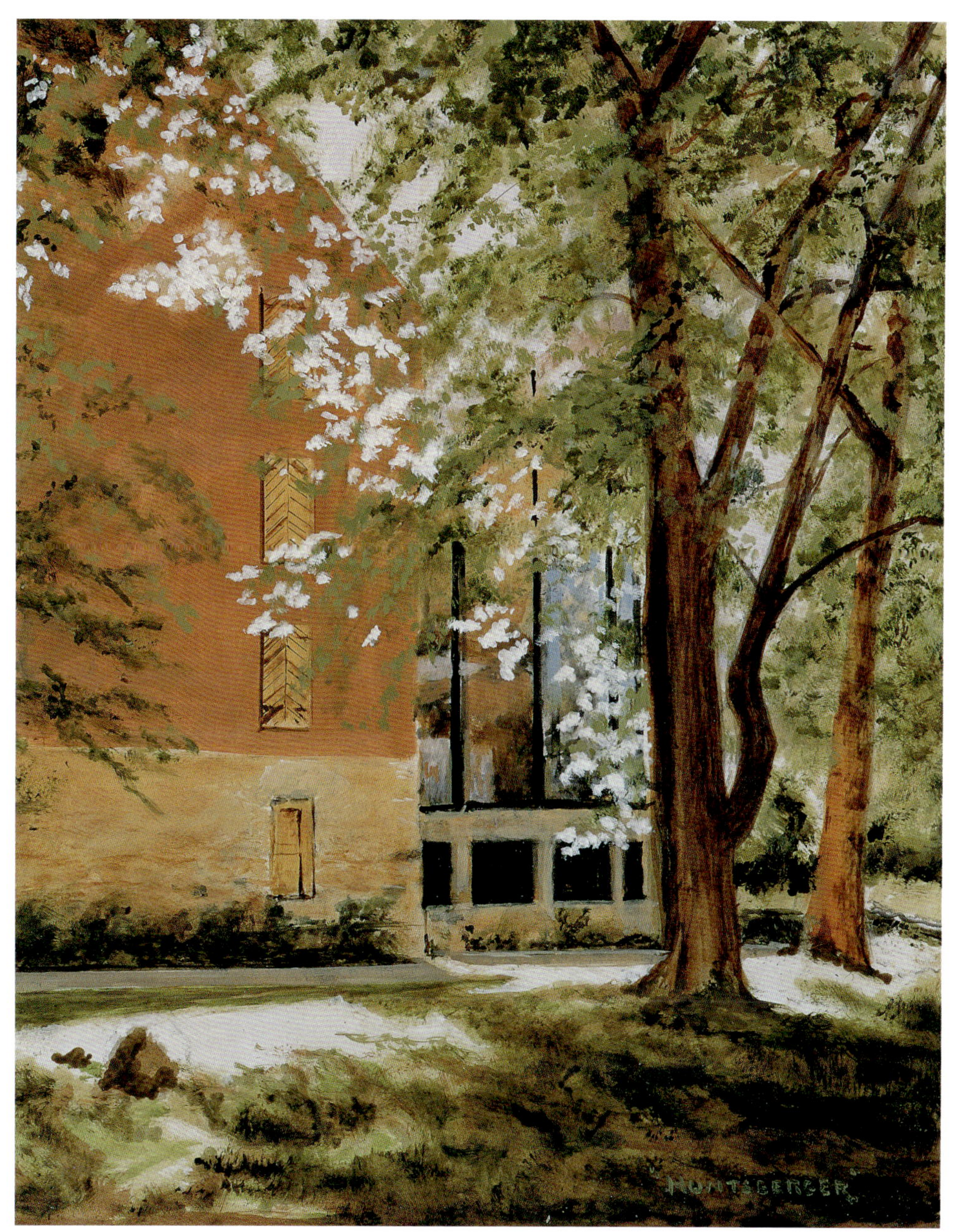
HUNTSBERGER

The Millstone

This particular millstone has been made into a table. Located in the creek-side garden of the Brandywine River Museum, it provides a popular climbing spot for children. Millstones are icons in the Brandywine Valley, where many have become stepping stones and fountains.

Millstones were essential to the success of Brandywine millers and were an important example of early American engineering technology. In very early days millstones were hewn from single slabs of sandstone, which was plentiful upstream in Berks County, Pennsylvania. Some stones were carelessly finished and of uneven thickness; some were not truly round. Early millstones were left flat, so the pores in the stone determined flour quality. Uneven pores produced uneven or poor quality flour.

In 1796 Oliver Evans obtained a patent on his improved method of millstone manufacture. Rather than a single slab of sandstone, Evans used pieces of small French burr stone carefully fit together. Cemented and dressed with plaster of Paris, Evans's millstones were truly round and carefully balanced. Iron hoops with wooden pegs secured the outer edges to withstand the centrifugal force of the revolving wheel. Rather than depend on the stone's natural pores for flour quality, Evans selected stone without pores, assembled the millstone, and then hand-cut furrows into it. The angle of the cutting edge in the furrow assured the quality of the flour.

The best burr stones were approximately one-foot square and imported from the La Ferte-sous-Jouarre quarries in France. During the War of 1812 the embargo forced Evans to search for another supply, and he found good American stones in Virginia, New York, and Ohio. An advertisement of that period said that Oliver Evans made burr millstones of American burr and warranted them as thicker and longer lasting than French stones.

One of my artist colleagues has counseled me to simplify—simplify! While visiting the Brandywine River Museum, I noticed the beauty of the millstone table and its shadow cast by a bright sun. A simple subject, certainly, but I think also an effective one. Counsel heard.

10" x 8" Oil on board 2001 Frank Jenkins

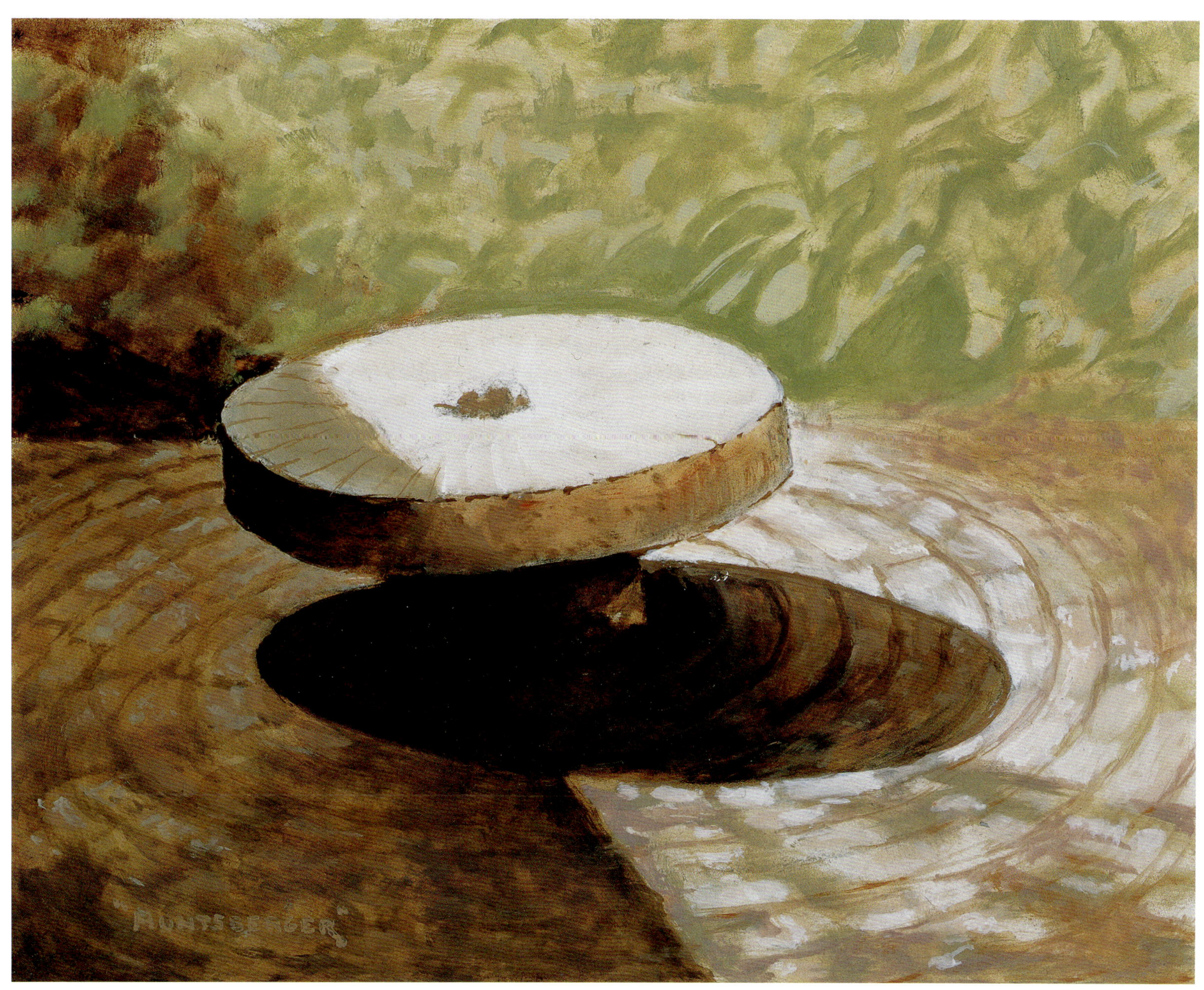
HUNTSBERGER

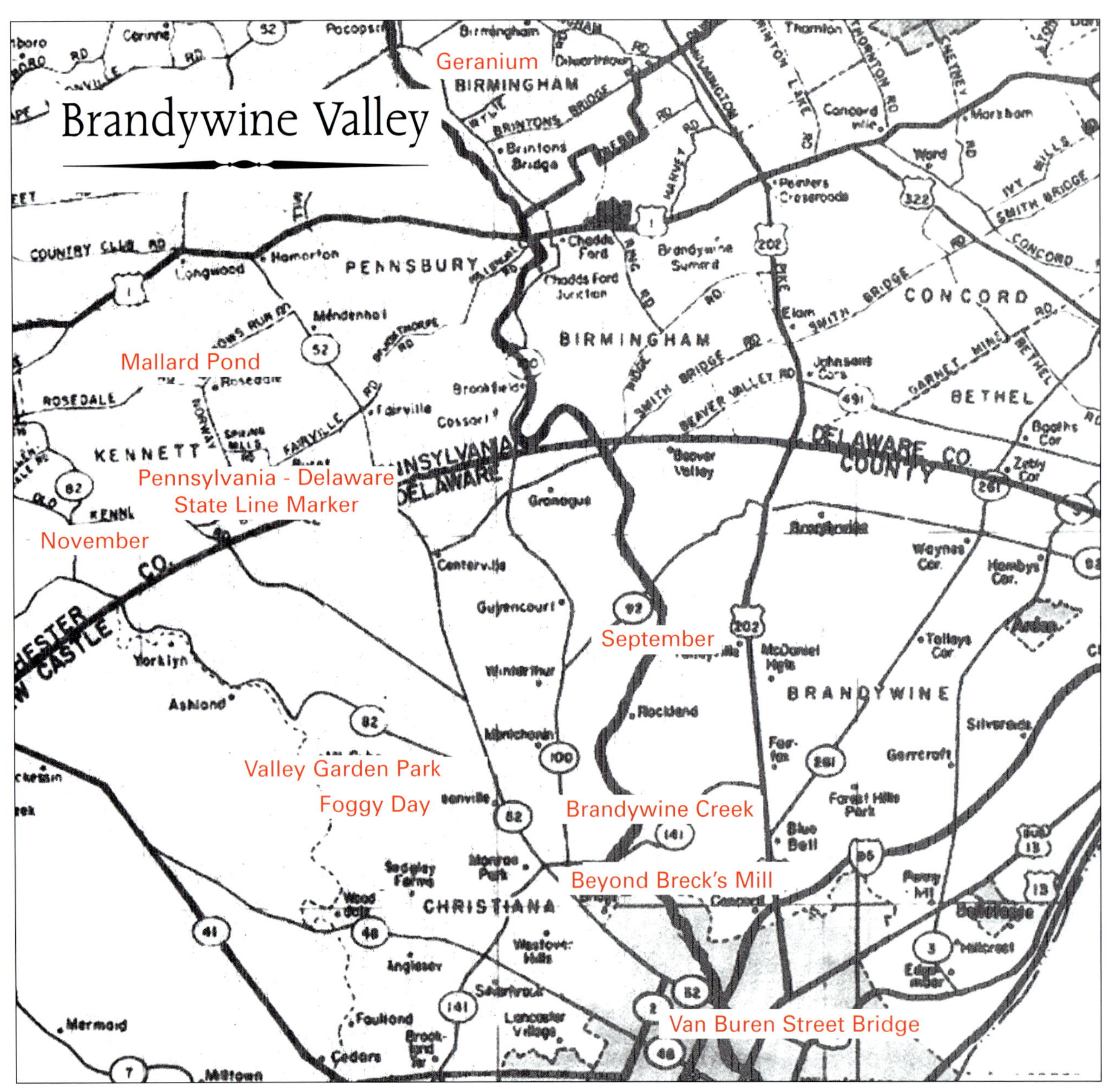
Brandywine Valley
Geranium
Mallard Pond
Pennsylvania - Delaware State Line Marker
November
September
Valley Garden Park
Foggy Day
Brandywine Creek
Beyond Breck's Mill
Van Buren Street Bridge
BIRMINGHAM
PENNSBURY
CONCORD
BETHEL
KENNETT
DELAWARE CO. COUNTY
BRANDYWINE
CHRISTIANA

Chapter Two

Brandywine Valley Landscapes

Today artists still find grand vistas to paint because great stretches of the land along the Brandywine River look much as they did in the days before the settlers.

The curved line in the middle of the map on the opposite page is the state borderline between Pennsylvania and Delaware. This arc forms a unique political boundary—the only semicircular border in the world.

In 1701 surveyors Isaac Taylor and Thomas Pierson marked the line to separate the lower three counties of Pennsylvania from the rest of the colony. They established the line to arc west from the Delaware River for 120 degrees or one-third of a circle, with a twelve-mile radius from the British courthouse in New Castle. When separated from Pennsylvania, the Three Lower Counties became the colony of Delaware. They received the right to a separate assembly, which first met in 1704.

The western end of Twelve-Mile Circle is near the point of origin of the Mason-Dixon Line, which marks the corner of the borders between Pennsylvania, Delaware, and Maryland. Although the Mason-Dixon Line is closely associated with the Civil War as the border between the north and the south, it was drawn nearly 100 years earlier to settle disputes over poorly defined property descriptions written into seventeenth-century royal grants.

In 1632 King Charles I of England gave George Calvert the colony of Maryland. In 1682 King Charles II of England granted William Penn the land that became Pennsylvania and the Delmarva Peninsula, which contains what is today the Eastern Shore of Maryland, the entire state of Delaware, and a small portion of the state of Virginia. Because the boundaries defined in the royal grants were so unclear, border disputes arose. After years of wrangling, of seeking justice in the British courts, and finally obtaining a ruling by England's chief justice in 1750, the Calvert and Penn families agreed that the boundary between southern Pennsylvania and northern Maryland should lie fifteen miles south of Philadelphia. Then they ordered a survey.

Colonial surveyors were not qualified to attempt this difficult task, so English surveyors Charles Mason and Jeremiah Dixon were hired in 1763. They began their task by determining the exact location of Philadelphia. The Mason-Dixon Line established the northern and eastern borders of Maryland.

The gap between the end of the Twelve-Mile Circle and the Mason-Dixon point of origin created a small wedge of land in the northwest corner of Delaware that wasn't under the arc. In 1892 surveyors extended the Mason-Dixon Line east from its point of origin to the Twelve-Mile Circle to form the "Top of the Wedge."

All of the surveyors set markers along their lines. Many of those markers have disappeared, but one is still in full view near the east shoulder of Kennett Pike (Route 52) at the Pennsylvania-Delaware border.

Brandywine Creek

Did the name "Brandywine" derive from a shipwreck or a man's name? Early land records show that Andrew Brandwin owned two hundred acres of land along the creek near the present day Market Street Bridge in Wilmington, Delaware.

When Brandwin sold the land in 1670, the deed described this parcel as *"lyeing and being to ye South of Brainwend Kill or Creeke."* In succeeding deeds for land along the creek, the spelling changes gradually until "Brandywine" is established for official records and found on charts and maps as well.

Long after Andrew Brandwin was gone and forgotten, the discovery of the old hulk of an overturned vessel rotting in the Christina River near the mouth of the Brandywine gave credence to the legend that a Dutch captain lost a cargo of brandy and wine when his ship overturned in a storm—thus contributing the name Brandywine to the creek.

Just north of the Henry Clay Mill a sycamore arcs gracefully across the creek.
I chose this spot for my first painting of the Brandywine.

20" x 16" Oil on canvas 1995

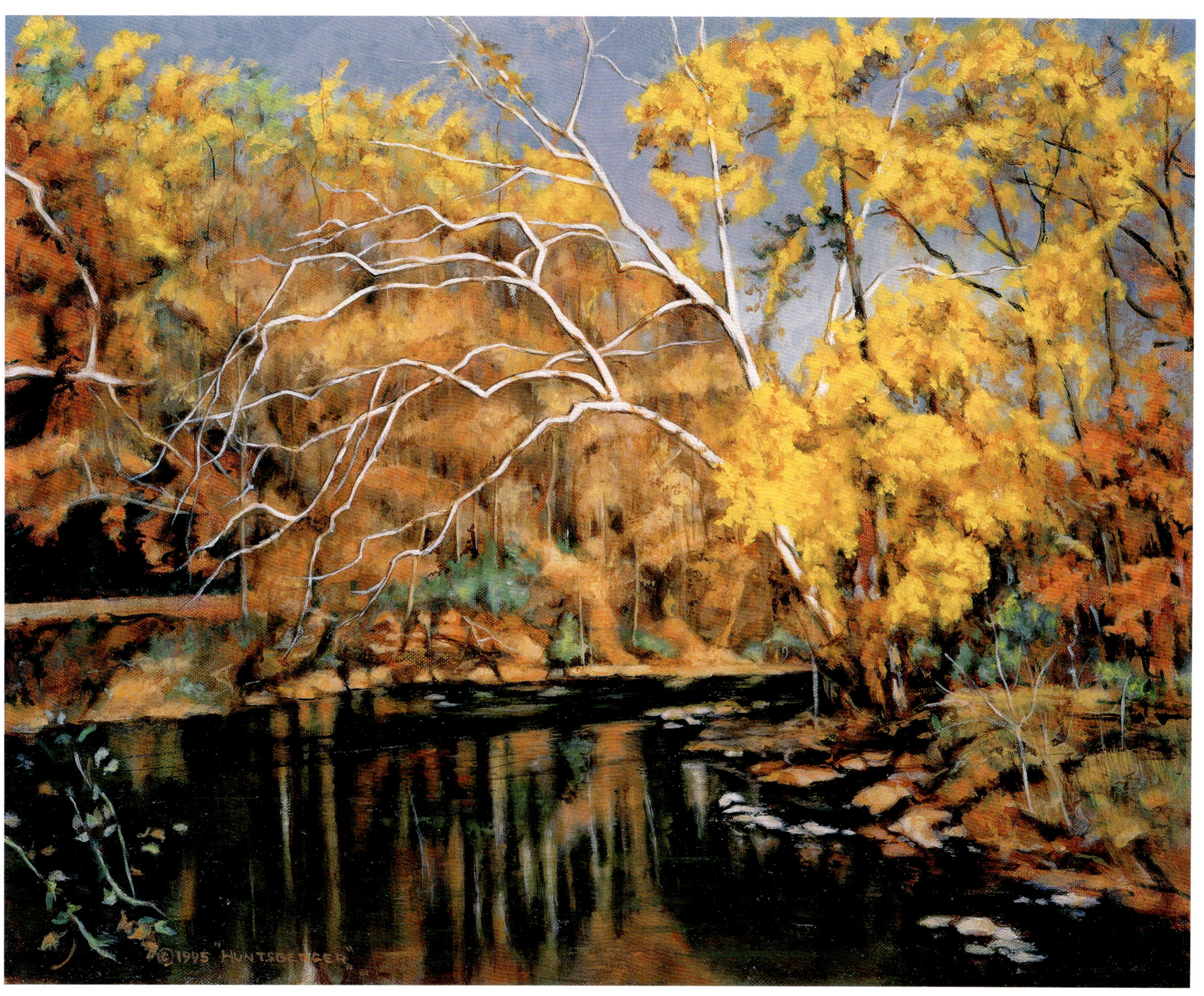
©1995

Van Buren Street Bridge

(Brandywine Creek II)

The Van Buren Street Bridge was built to link two parts of Brandywine Park in Wilmington, Delaware. The 286-foot-long span is unique because it is the only example of an eight-span, filled-solid spandrel, concrete-arch bridge. The original 1906 drawings for the 353-foot-long bridge show two different forms of historic steel beam reinforcement: latticed rolled I-beam and bar reinforcement. The two-lane bridge was highly embellished from its concrete substructure to its ornate balustrade. These decorations were removed during repairs.

The concrete arch encases a forty-eight-inch-diameter pipe to carry water across the Brandywine from the Porter Reservoir on Concord Pike to the filter station at Sixteenth and Market streets. The cost of the combined highway bridge and aqueduct was $40,000 in 1906. The bridge was repaired in 1958, 1970, and 1999 at total costs far exceeding the original price.

The nationally prominent Concrete Steel Engineering Company of New York City built the Van Buren Street Bridge. In the ten years between 1894 to 1904, the firm had constructed more than three hundred concrete bridges across the United States.

This Wilmington bridge has been a favorite subject for many of our local artists. When I found this site, I decided to join the crowd and try my hand.

24" x 18" Oil on canvas 2001 Collection of Mrs. David Craven

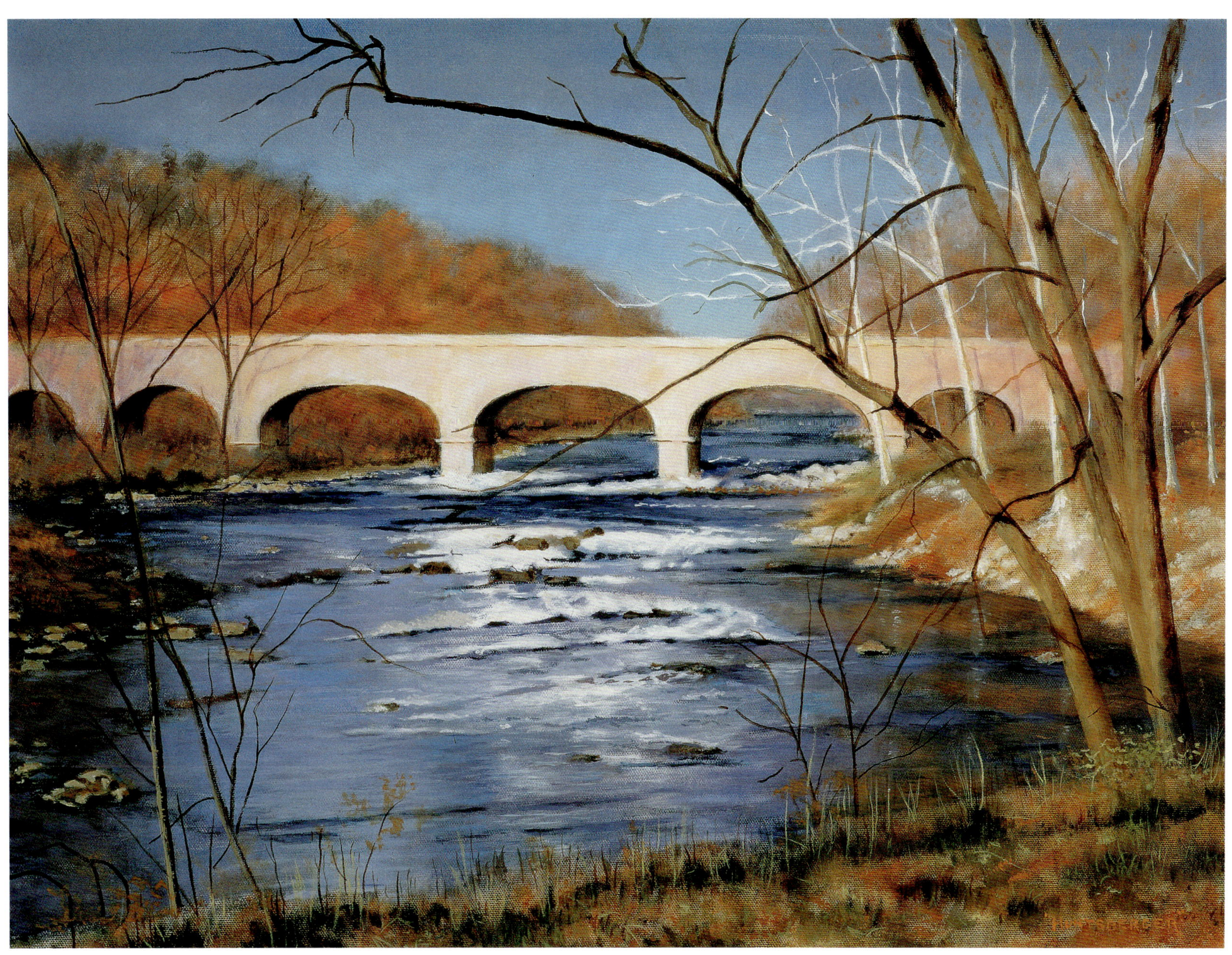

Geranium

This little corner of a beautifully restored old stone barn near the Brandywine caught my eye. In the window was a single geranium plant. The barn is a couple of miles north of Andrew Wyeth's home and I was reminded of his painting, Marsh Hawk in which the hawk is a tiny figure in the background. As the geranium was so obscure, I decided to call this painting Geranium.

20" x 16" Oil on canvas 1997 Private collection

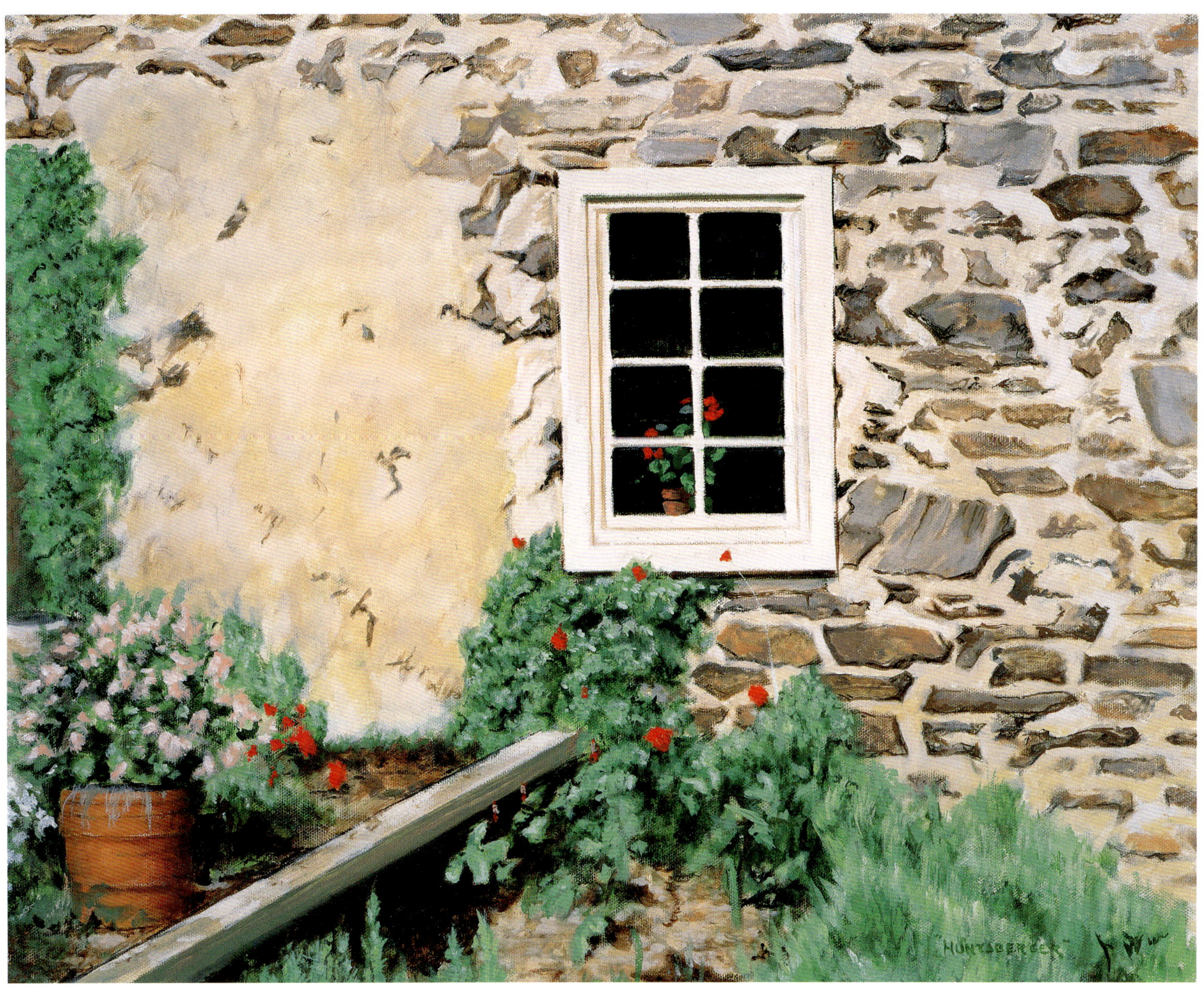

Chester County Farm

Many times each year Janet and I drive to enjoy the beauty of our Brandywine Valley. Often we encounter scenes like this farm in Chester County. I liked the compact grouping of buildings and the rather strong diagonal element.

20" x 16" Oil on canvas 2003

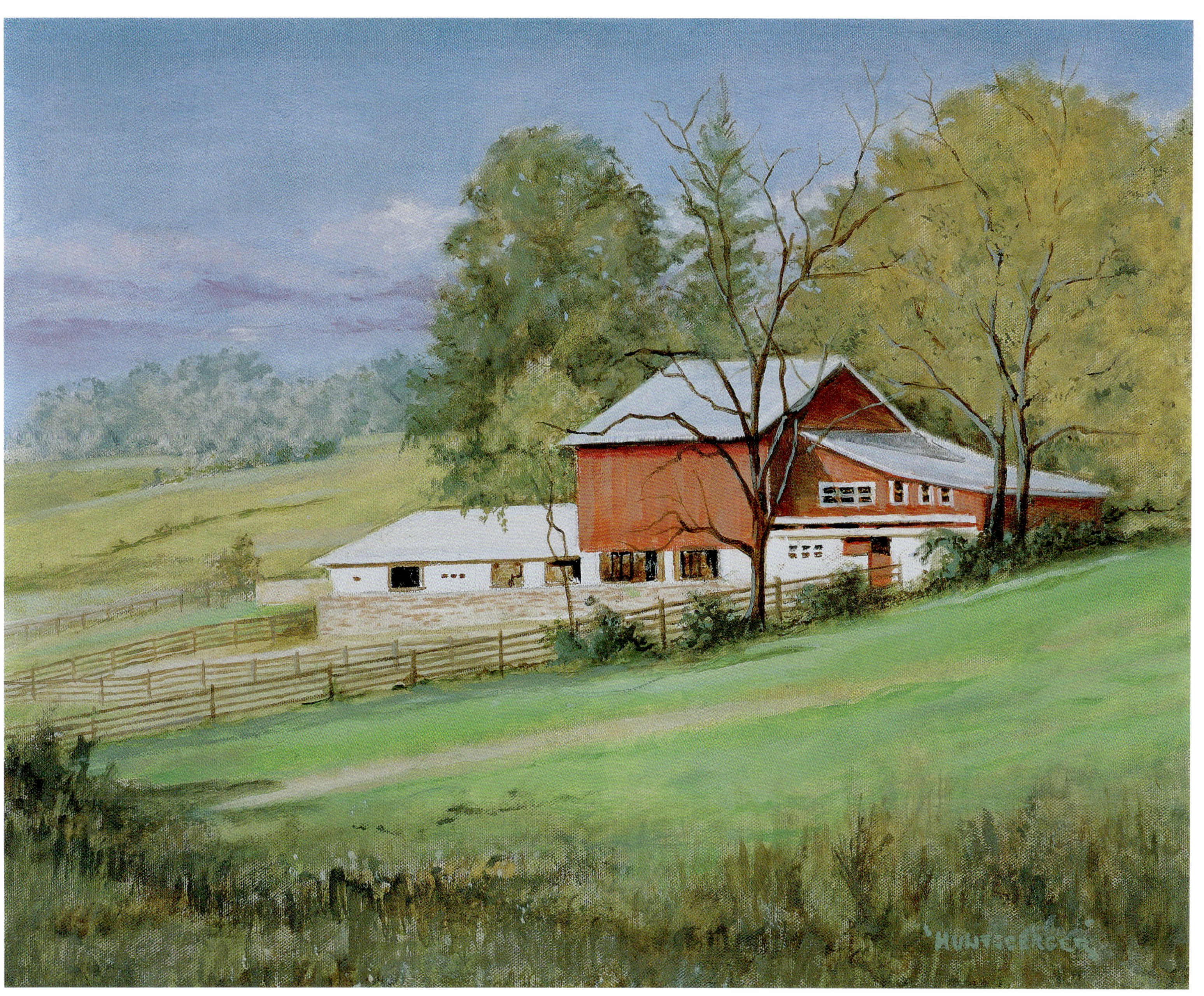

Mallard Pond

This is a scene I see often as we pass it frequently driving along Bayard Road. It seemed especially inviting on the day that I stopped to take reference photos for my painting. Actually there were many Canada geese there at the time, but I thought Mallard Pond would be a more appealing title for the painting. The trees near the pond have grown so much that this view is no longer seen from the road.

36” x 24” Oil on canvas 1993 Corporate Collection

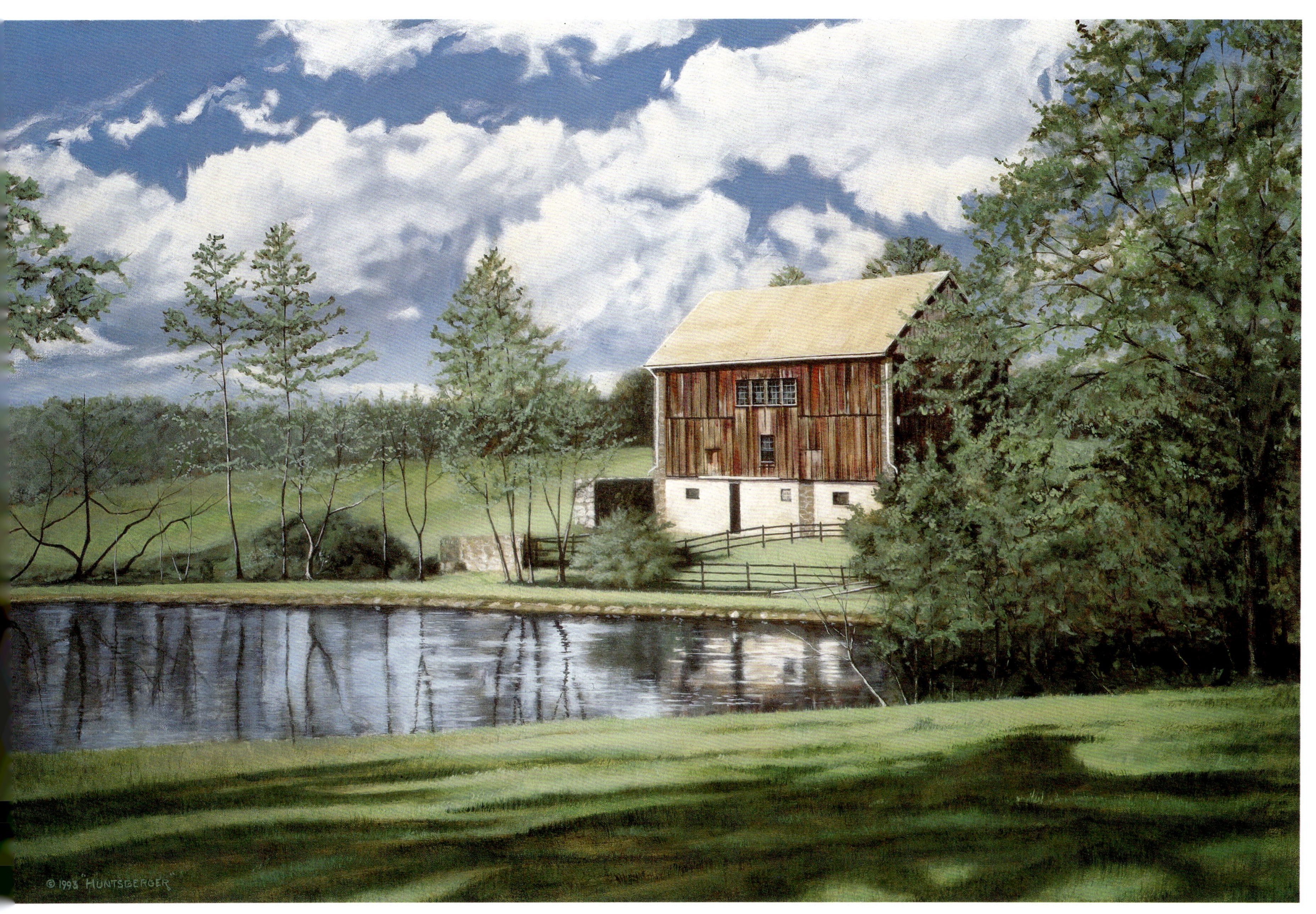
© 1993 "HUNTSBERGER"

November

This beautiful stone house is a couple of miles from my home. I have taken quite a few liberties here. I left out two wooden structures, which I thought detracted from its beauty. I added the well for pictorial balance and the burning leaves to suggest a human presence. When this oil painting was on exhibit during a one-man show, a longtime resident of the area approached me. He said that when he was a boy the well had, in fact, been right where I placed it.

48” x 36” Oil on canvas 1994 Corporate Collection

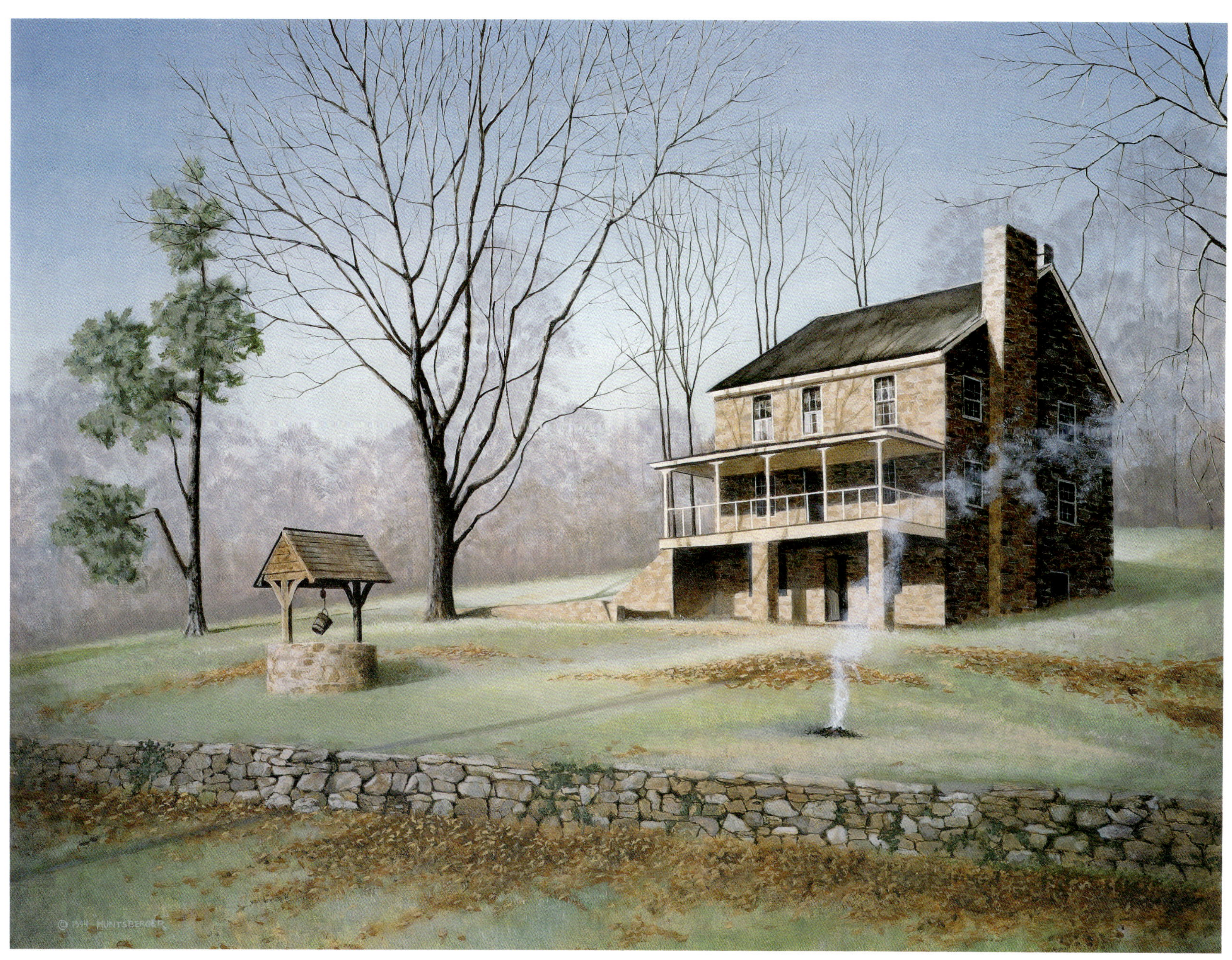
© 1994 HUNTSBERGER

Beyond Breck's Mill

This is the view of the tower on Walker's Mill (left) on the east bank of the Brandywine and of the top of Rockford Tower (right) from the north end of Breck's Mill on the west bank of the Brandywine. This view is visible only when the trees have no leaves.

In the early nineteenth century Alfred Victor du Pont acquired Breck's Mill to manufacture woolen fabric. Later it became the site for informal du Pont family parties, a practice space for a du Pont family orchestra, and an arena for amateur dramatics staged for charity. During World War I the old stone building was the Hagley Community Center for munitions workers. Now the well-maintained Breck's Mill contains the Montchanin Post Office, an art gallery, and a sculptor's studio. Walker's Mill was a woolen mill during the nineteenth century.

Rockford Tower is a Wilmington, Delaware, landmark in Rockford Park. William P. Bancroft donated the park to the city of Wilmington as part of a plan to prevent industrial spoliation of the Brandywine within the city limits.

It is surprising that these landmarks, separated by sizable hills and nearly three-quarters of a mile apart, can be seen in a single view. I decided to paint this curiosity.

18" x 18" Oil on canvas 1998

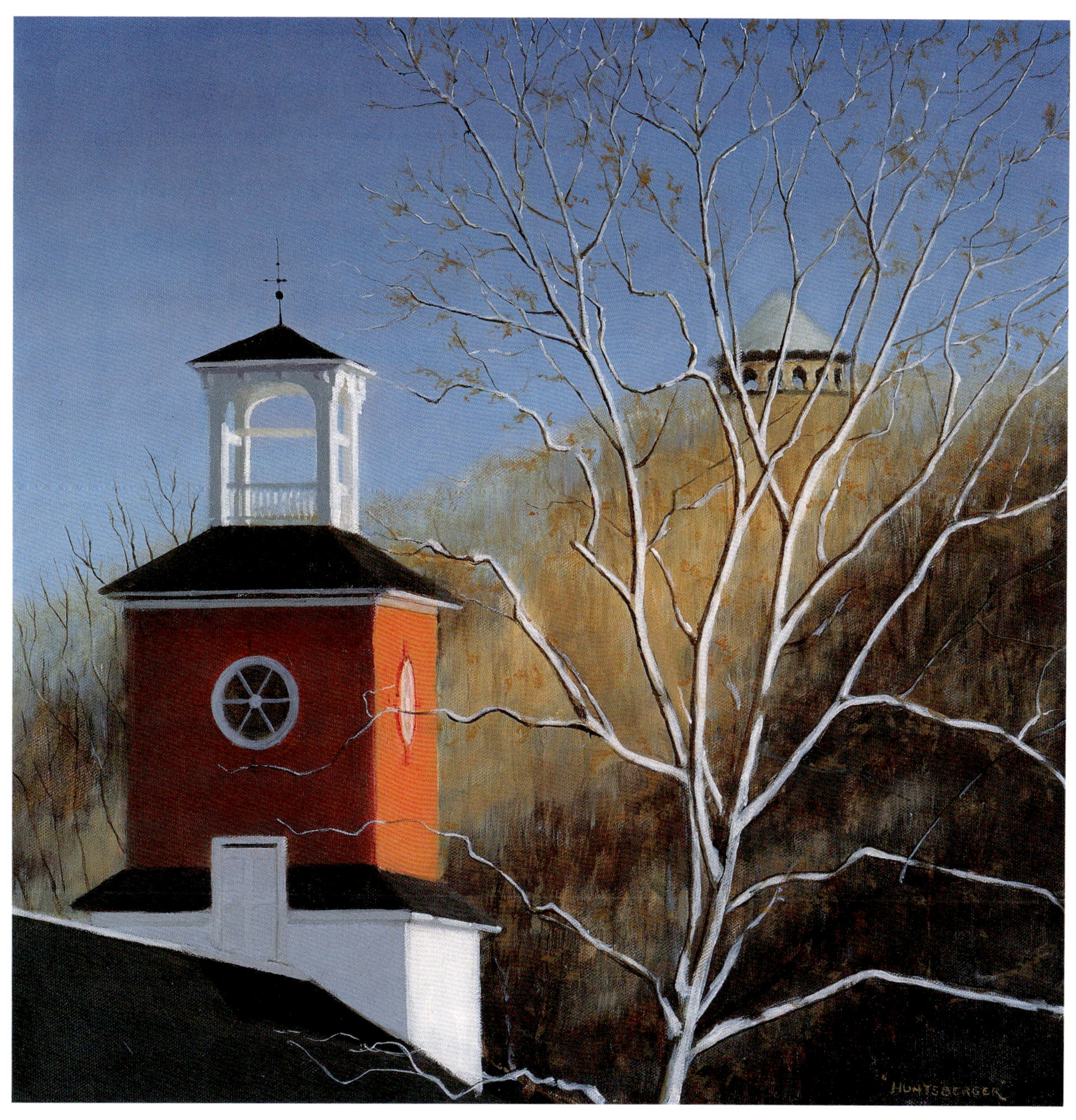
HUNTSBERGER

Brandywine Creek State Park

(September)

Lying five miles north of downtown Wilmington and two miles south of the Pennsylvania-Delaware state line, Brandywine Creek State Park offers gently rolling upland meadows, gentle to moderate slopes, wooded areas along the ridges, and a steep stream valley. The entrance road, parking lots, and nature center are the only modern intrusions in an intact late nineteenth-century pastoral scene.

Visitors can descend from the nature center down a fairly steep path to the swampy floodplain of the Brandywine. Old-growth cottonwood and sycamore trees shade the creek. When the creek-side path ascends from the river, the view shown in September is visible. This is a huge grassy hill with a six-foot-tall stone wall along the top. A popular Frisbee course is laid out on the brow of the hill. This spot is about a one-mile trek to the parking lot near the nature center.

As Janet and I started up the path from the Brandywine Creek I was taken by the remarkable, strong diagonal of the path leading to the clump of trees and stone wall, which provide a natural point of interest.

36" x 24" Oil on canvas 1992 Corporate Collection

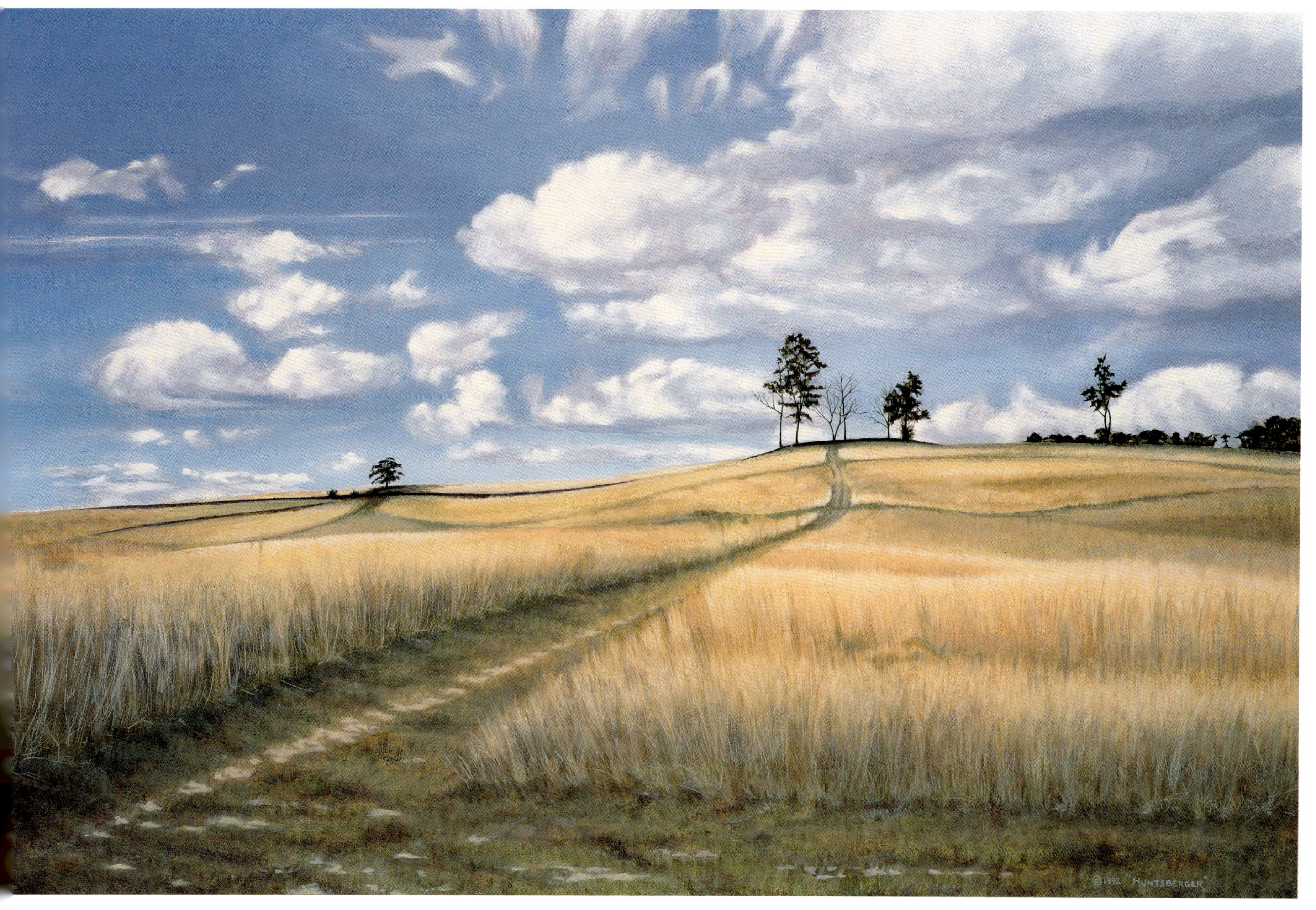
©1992 "HUNTSBERGER"

Valley Garden Park

(Springtime)

Approximately one-half mile west of its intersection with Kennett Pike, Route 82 passes the paved, gated private lane at the entrance to Valley Garden Park. Just beyond is the spacious parking lot built after Ellen Wheelwright gave the park to the city of Wilmington in memory of her mother, Mrs. T. Coleman du Pont.

Valley Garden Park is a quarter-mile long and several hundred yards wide, bounded by wooded ridges on either side. Built along a small brook that cut a deep gully through what was previously a barnyard and pasture, Valley Garden Park contains many flowering bulbs, shrubs, and trees transplanted in 1930 from Mrs. T. Coleman du Pont's Old Mill Garden, which was later submerged by the Hoopes Reservoir. The brook is dammed at intervals to create small pools, which are bordered with irises.

The paved driveway that encircles the park is a pleasant walking path for visitors while the steeply sloped sidewalk and sturdy steps between the parking lot and the garden provide a good workout for hardier souls. Popular with teen-agers, young families, and retired people, well-maintained Valley Garden Park is one of the Brandywine Valley's most frequented showplaces.

The park is about two miles from our home, so we visit often. It is delightful throughout the year. I have painted several oils of the park. This one displays the springtime show of beauty.

20" x 16" Oil on canvas 2001 Collection of Mrs. David Craven

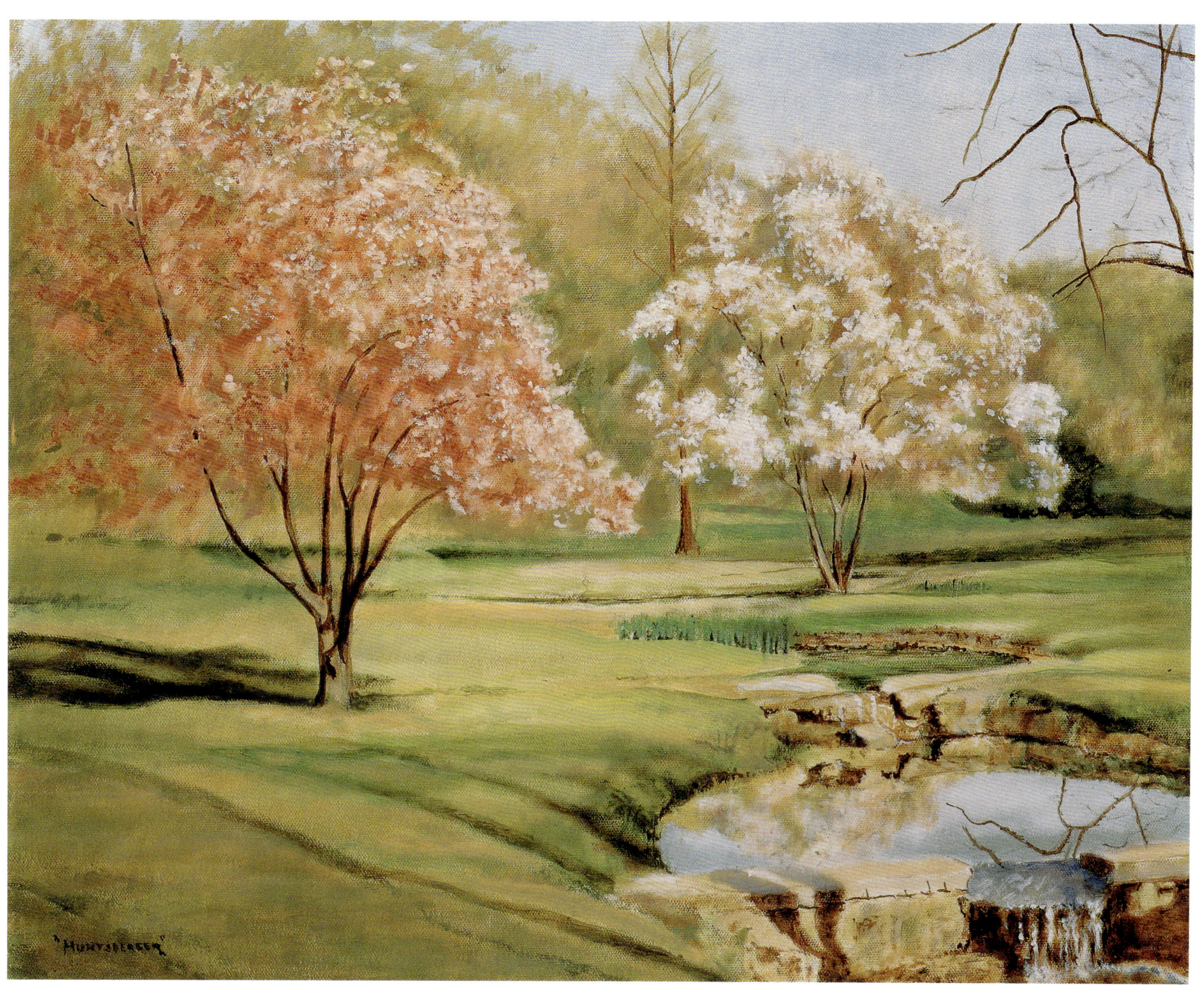
"HUNTSBERGER"

Foggy Day

The mystery of a foggy day is something I have often wanted to paint. This scene at Valley Garden Park is my initial attempt to capture such a day.

14" x 10" Oil on canvas 1997 Collection of Cheryl Cantrell

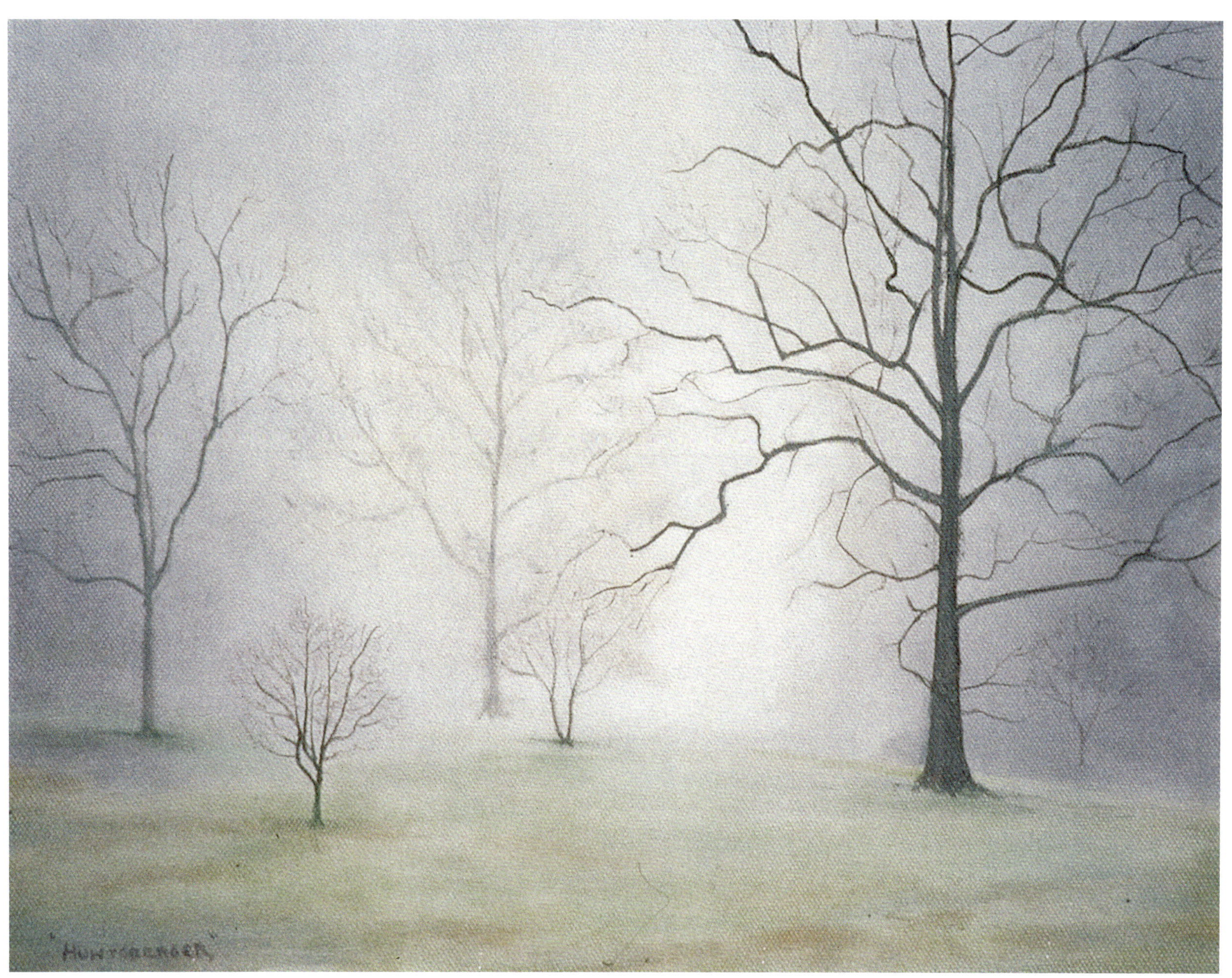

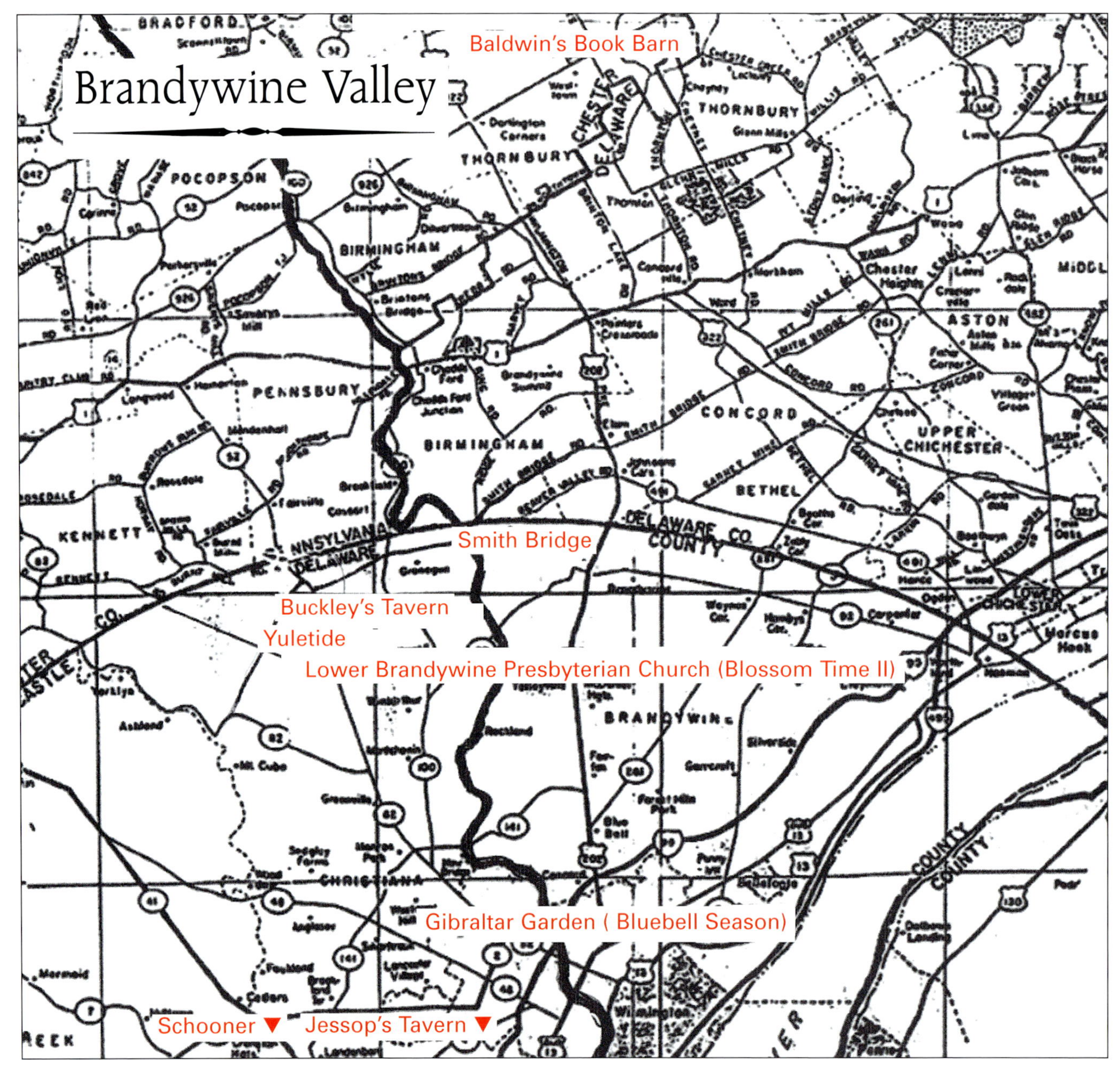

Brandywine Valley
Baldwin's Book Barn
Smith Bridge
Buckley's Tavern
Yuletide
Lower Brandywine Presbyterian Church (Blossom Time II)
Gibraltar Garden (Bluebell Season)
Schooner ▼
Jessop's Tavern ▼
BRADFORD
POCOPSON
THORNBURY
BIRMINGHAM
PENNSBURY
KENNETT
CONCORD
BETHEL
ASTON
UPPER CHICHESTER
DELAWARE CO
CHRISTIANA

Chapter Three

Landmarks

Baldwin's Book Barn

Located on Route 52 on the southwest edge of West Chester, Pennsylvania, this rambling old barn is a magnet for readers. Filled with all types of books, Baldwin's Book Barn has been supplying fine used and rare books, manuscripts, and maps to Brandywine Valley families since 1948. The well-organized 300,000-volume collection is spread over five stories in a rustic 1822 dairy barn. Visitors are welcome to enjoy the comfy chairs while making their selections.

Here's the place to find first editions and volumes about local history as well as literature, history, and novels. Baldwin's offers fine paintings and prints, estate antiques, and other valued collectibles. Interior designers come to Baldwin's to purchase "books by the foot" for their clients' empty shelves. Theatrical set designers have borrowed books as well.

Baldwin's is right up to date so you can find them at www.bookbarn.com, but nothing compares to spending time in their barn. Baldwin's is everyone's destination on rainy days.

This is such a well-known attraction in the Brandywine Valley that I felt compelled to paint it.

20" x 16" Oil on canvas 2001 Collection of Mrs. David Craven

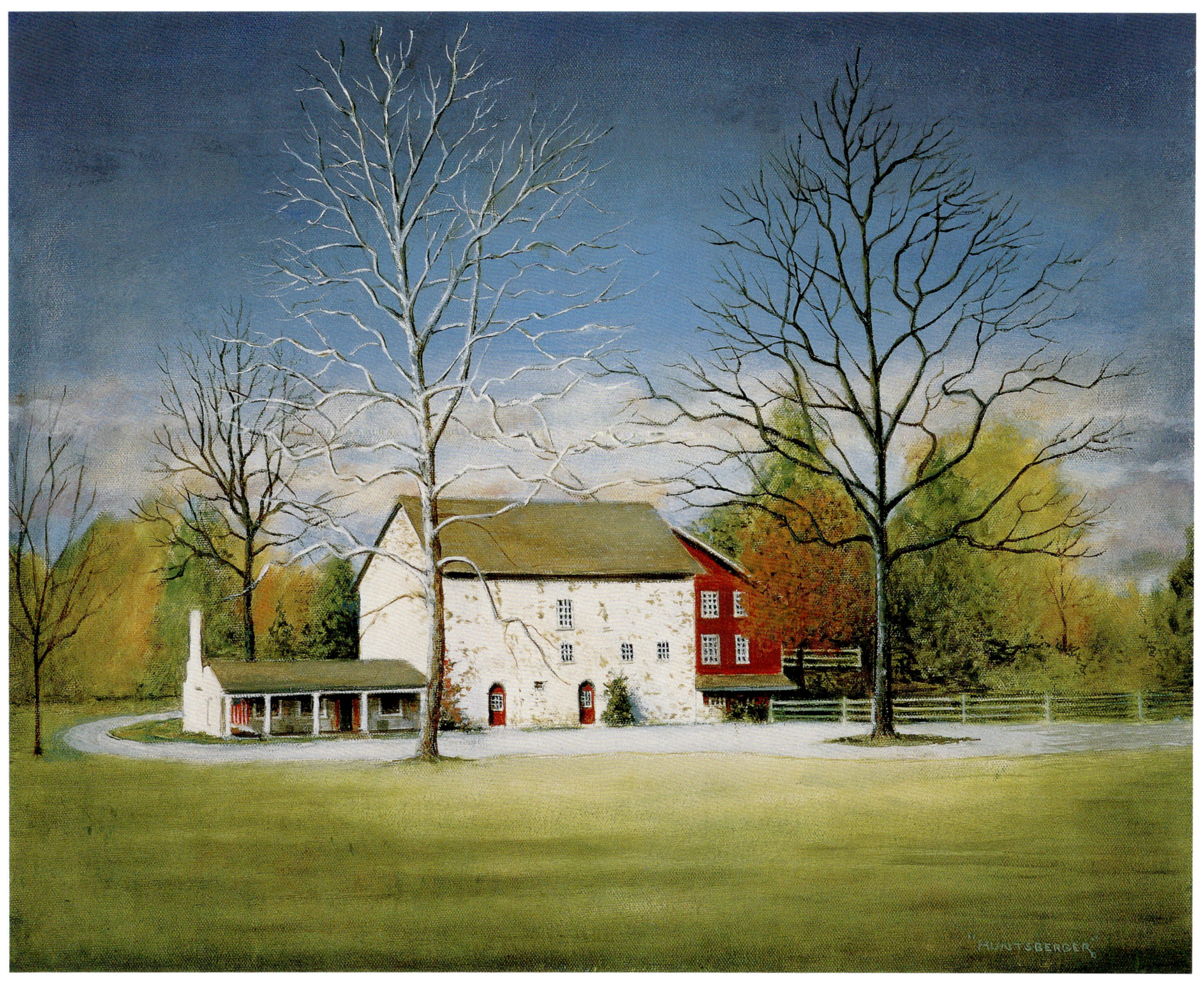
"HUNTSBERGER"

Smith Bridge

The original 1839 Smith Bridge was a one-lane covered wooden span across the Brandywine near Delaware's northern border with Pennsylvania. It was burned by vandals on Halloween 1961.

The second bridge was built without a cover. After forty years the roadbed was badly warped and deteriorated. The Delaware Department of Transportation plan was to build a modern-style two-lane replacement.

Local residents rallied to oppose the department's plan and were successful. They wanted to preserve the historic flavor of the area, which would have been impaired by a modern structure. This one-lane covered bridge, modeled after the 1839 original, was completed in 2002. The 145-foot span, built on the old piers, has new steel beams, wooden deck, and roof.

Local citizens are pleased with the new bridge because it retains the pastoral ambiance of the surrounding area while incorporating modern engineering and safety modifications. In May 2003 the New Castle County Review Board awarded the Centreville Civic Association a Historic Preservation Award for outstanding advocacy work on this project.

Over the years twenty-six covered bridges were built in Delaware. Most of them are now gone, for only two wooden covered bridges remain in the state today.

This is another of the well-known places within a mile or two of our home.
We use it frequently and feel fortunate to have this much beauty so readily accessible.

20" x 16" Oil on canvas 2003 Collection of Mrs. David Craven

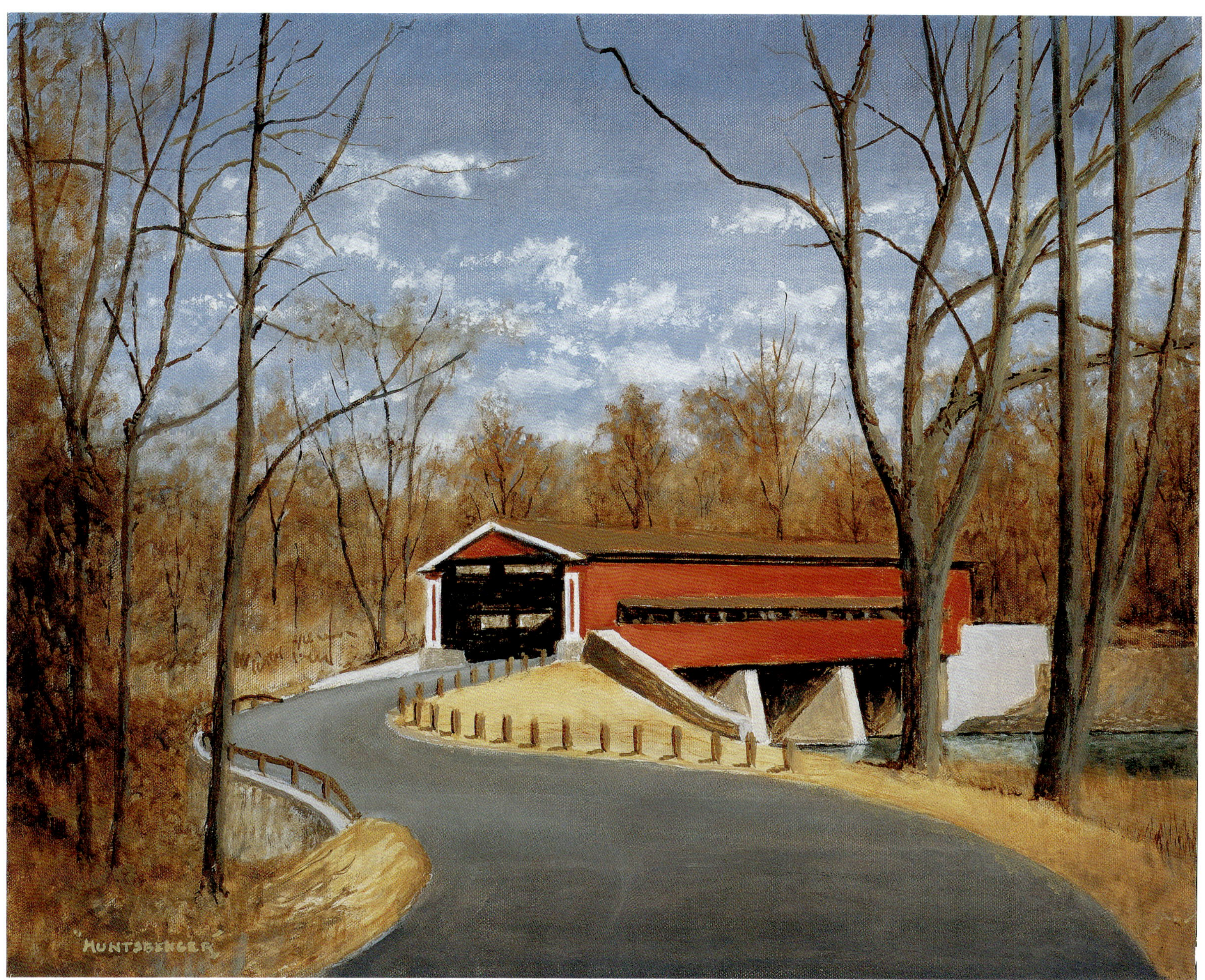
"HUNTSBERGER"

Buckley's Tavern

Buckley's Tavern, in the heart of Centreville, Delaware, looks as if it has been a stopping place for weary travelers since before the Revolutionary War. Looks can be deceiving!

Alan Buckley was the first proprietor of the tavern, opened in the 1960s when W. W. Laird purchased the building and surrounding property. Previously the place was used as a private residence, and the adjacent parking lot was the site of a wheelwright shop, then later, a filling station.

Buckley's Tavern houses a wine and spirits store, a taproom, and a restaurant. During pleasant weather a rooftop area is open for dining. Thursday night is a popular singles night at Buckley's as Centreville attracts throngs of people and parking space is at a premium.

I needed early morning light for Buckley's façade and also to avoid heavy traffic. People often comment that this doesn't look correct without parked cars lining the street. However it can look this way at times.

28" x 22" Oil on canvas 1991 Corporate Collection

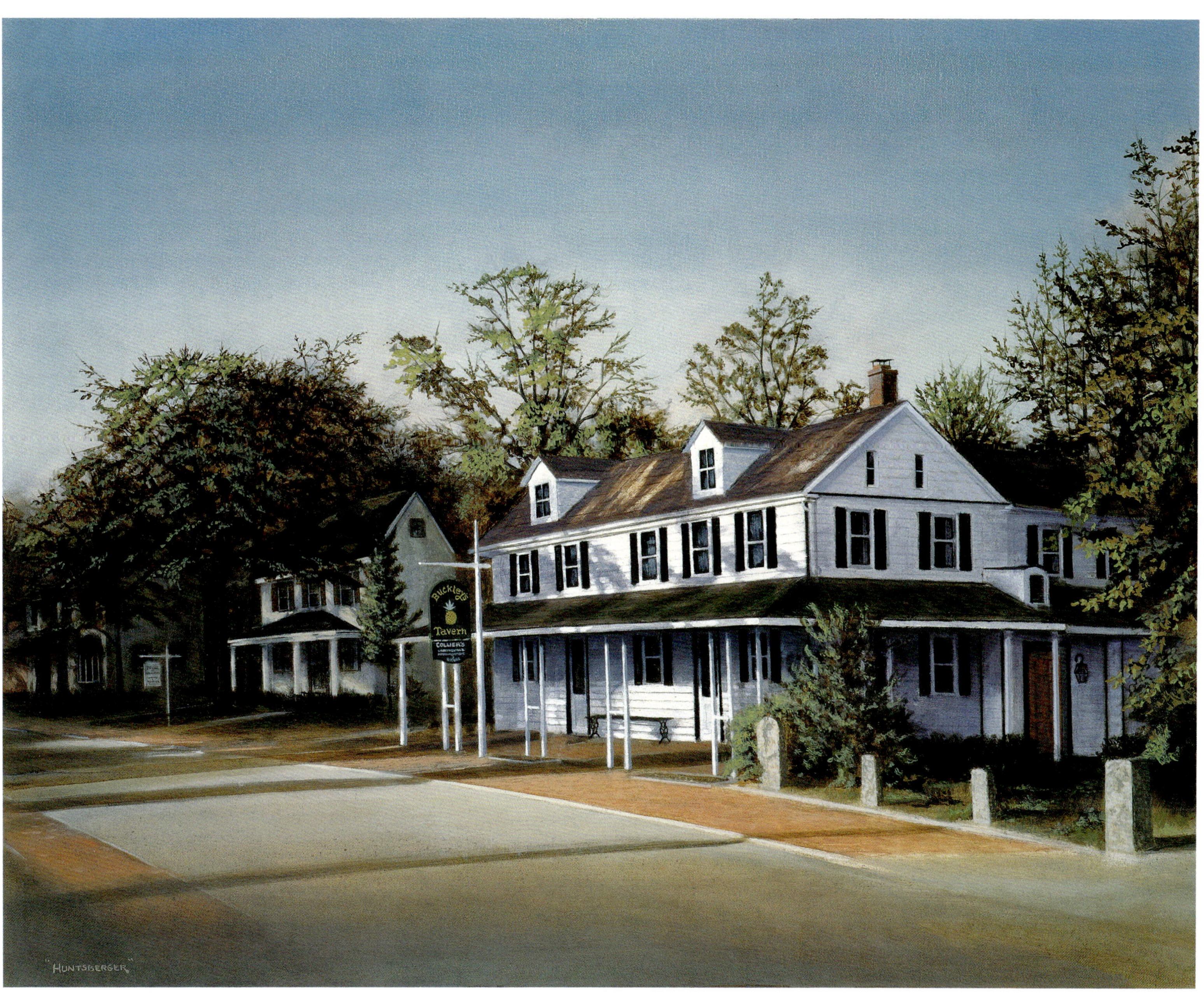
Buckley's
Tavern
COLLIER'S
"HUNTSBERGER"

Lower Brandywine Presbyterian Church

(Blossom Time II)

This Centreville, Delaware, church is one of the landmarks along the Kennett Pike. In 1720 the congregation organized and chose this site to build their church after a prolonged controversy. Some of the parishioners wanted it built on the west bank of the Brandywine; others wanted it on the east bank. The debate continued until a few years before the Revolutionary War when the original building, located in Pennsylvania, became unfit to use.

In 1774 a small log building was erected on the current church site. In 1859 the cornerstone for the present church was laid, and an addition to house the church school was added to the rear of the church in 1950.

Years ago the weeping cherry trees created a remarkable springtime display, which literally stopped traffic. Luckily I shot many slides during the 1970s that I used as references for this painting, because many of the old trees have fallen to wind and old age. The remaining trees show off well, if not with the old splendor. This church has much meaning for me because my first wife, Ardath, is buried in its cemetery. Years later Janet and I were married here.

48” x 36” Oil on canvas 2000

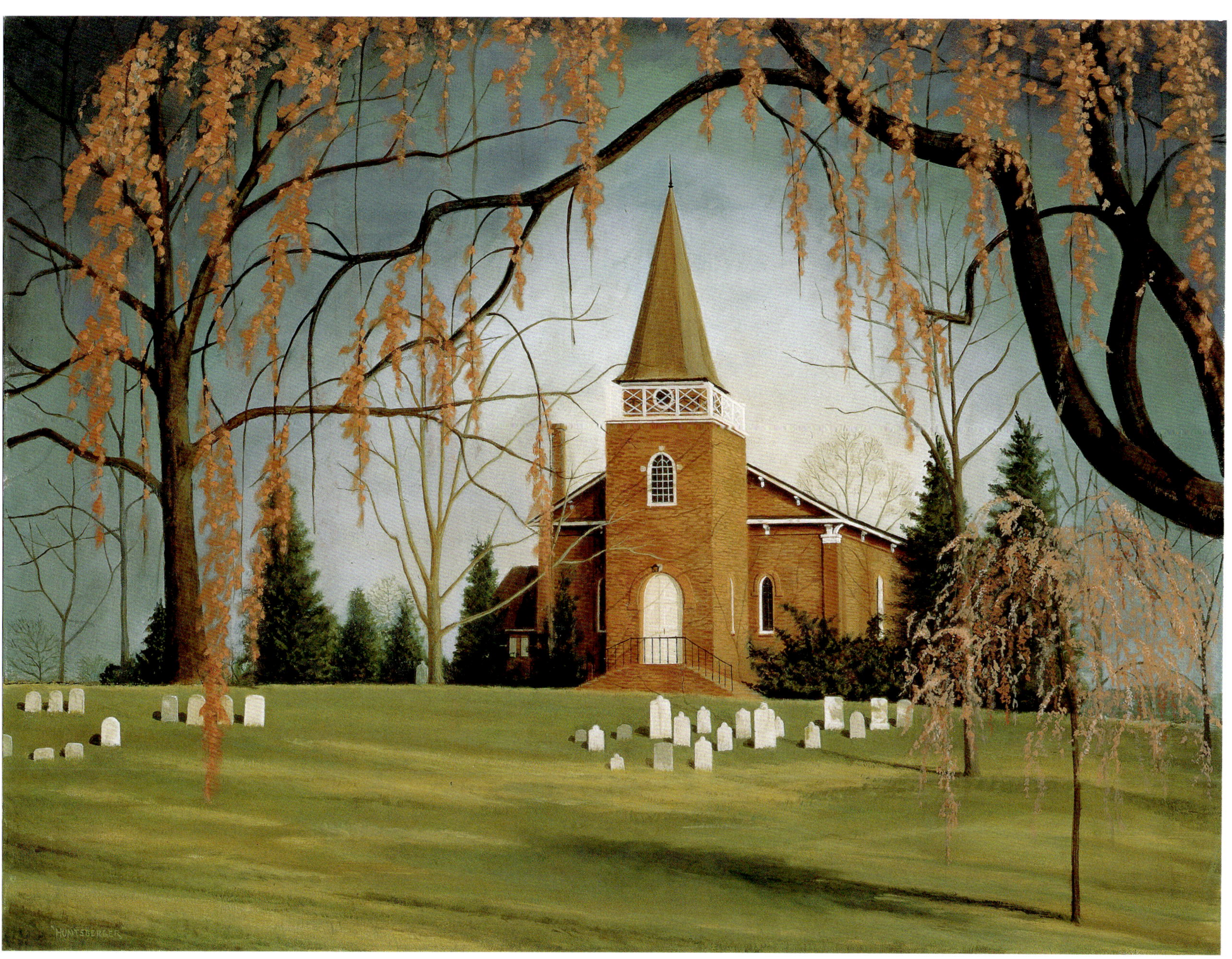
HUNTSBERGER

Yuletide

Every year a holiday wreath decorates Sylvester De Paulo's landmark barn on Route 52 in Centreville, Delaware. Fourteen feet in diameter, the wreath supports a bow containing sixty-five yards of ribbon.

This handsome barn is located on a ten-acre farm named "Maplebrook" for its quiet stream and the sugar maples lining the driveway. Scratched into its interior plaster are the date 1844, the names John Barton Clark and Benjamin Walker, and this inscription, *"Learn of me...be humble in these latter days."*

Each summer the barn is draped with a huge American flag. In 2001 after the September 11 tragedy, the flag remained on the barn until two weeks before Christmas.

Reflections in ponds, streams, or lakes always pique my interest. The little pond near the road allowed me to catch the barn and some background.

24" x 18" Oil on canvas 2000

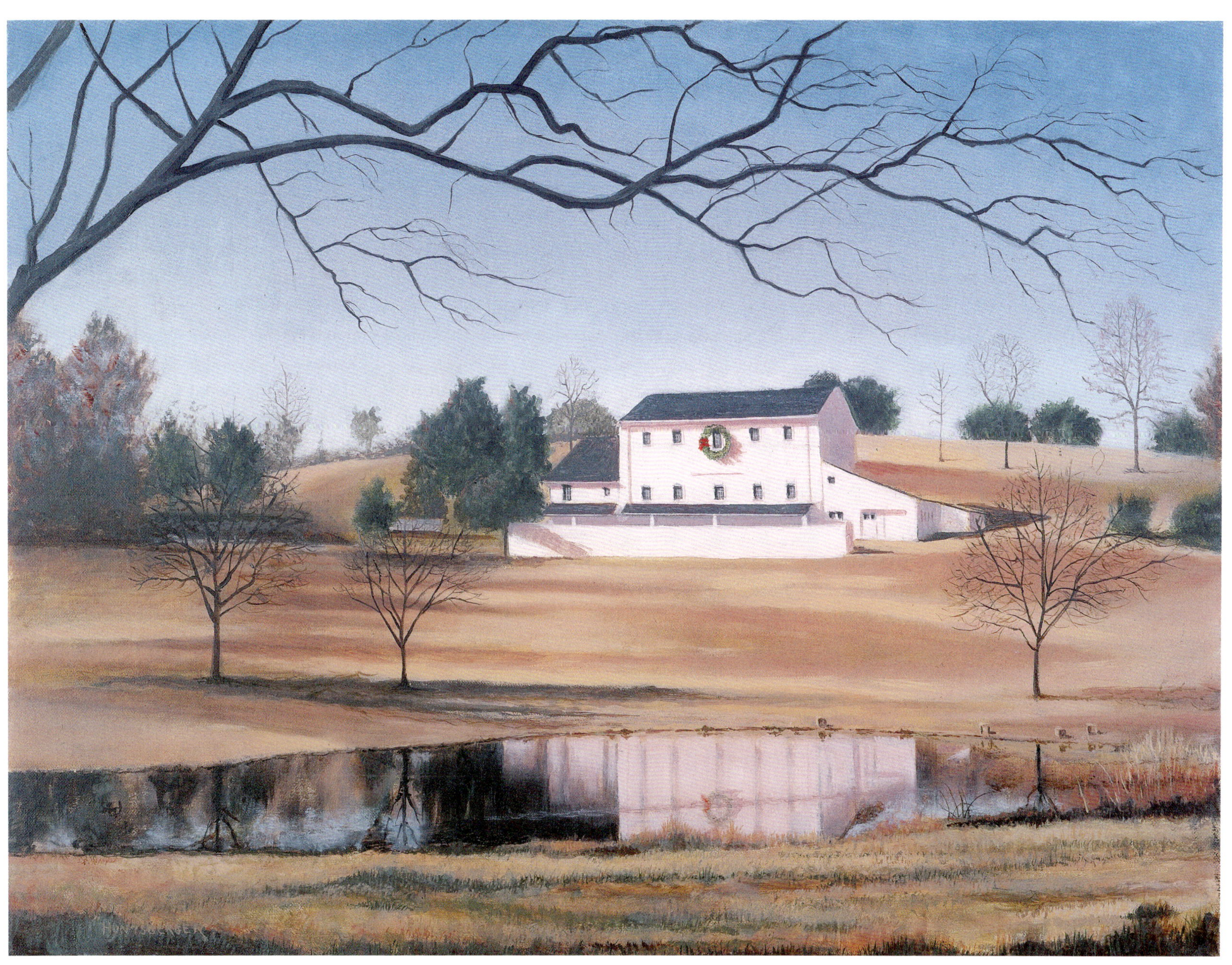

Gibraltar Garden

(Bluebell Season)

In 1844 John Rodney Brinckle built the huge stone mansion he christened Gibraltar because it stands on a high, rocky promontory. (The Brinckle family is also known as Brincklé and Brinkloes.) In 1909 the six-acre estate was purchased by Hugh Rodney Sharp and his wife, Isabella Mathieu du Pont Sharp. The Sharps invited Marian Cruger Coffin, the accomplished American landscape architect, to design Gibraltar's formal gardens.

Developed between 1916 and 1923, the gardens contain a series of rooms and terraces built along the slope of the land. The formal gardens were placed on flat land at the base of the promontory, and the remainder of the estate was on sloped English-landscape-style lawns.

In 1995 Preservation Delaware, Inc., the state of Delaware, and the property owners formed a unique public-private partnership to protect the unoccupied estate permanently from development. The property was then donated to Preservation Delaware, Inc.

During the 1990s a team of landscapers used the original plans and Coffin's specified plant materials to restore the Marian Cruger Coffin Gardens at Gibraltar to their original splendor. The landscapers made minor modifications to allow access for visitors with disabilities. In 1998 the property was placed on the National Register of Historic Places, and in 1999 the gardens opened to the public.

The patches of light filtering through the trees and lighting the curving path leading past the bench afforded a nice composition for this section of the bluebell garden.

20" x 16" Oil on canvas 2002 Collection of Mrs. David Craven

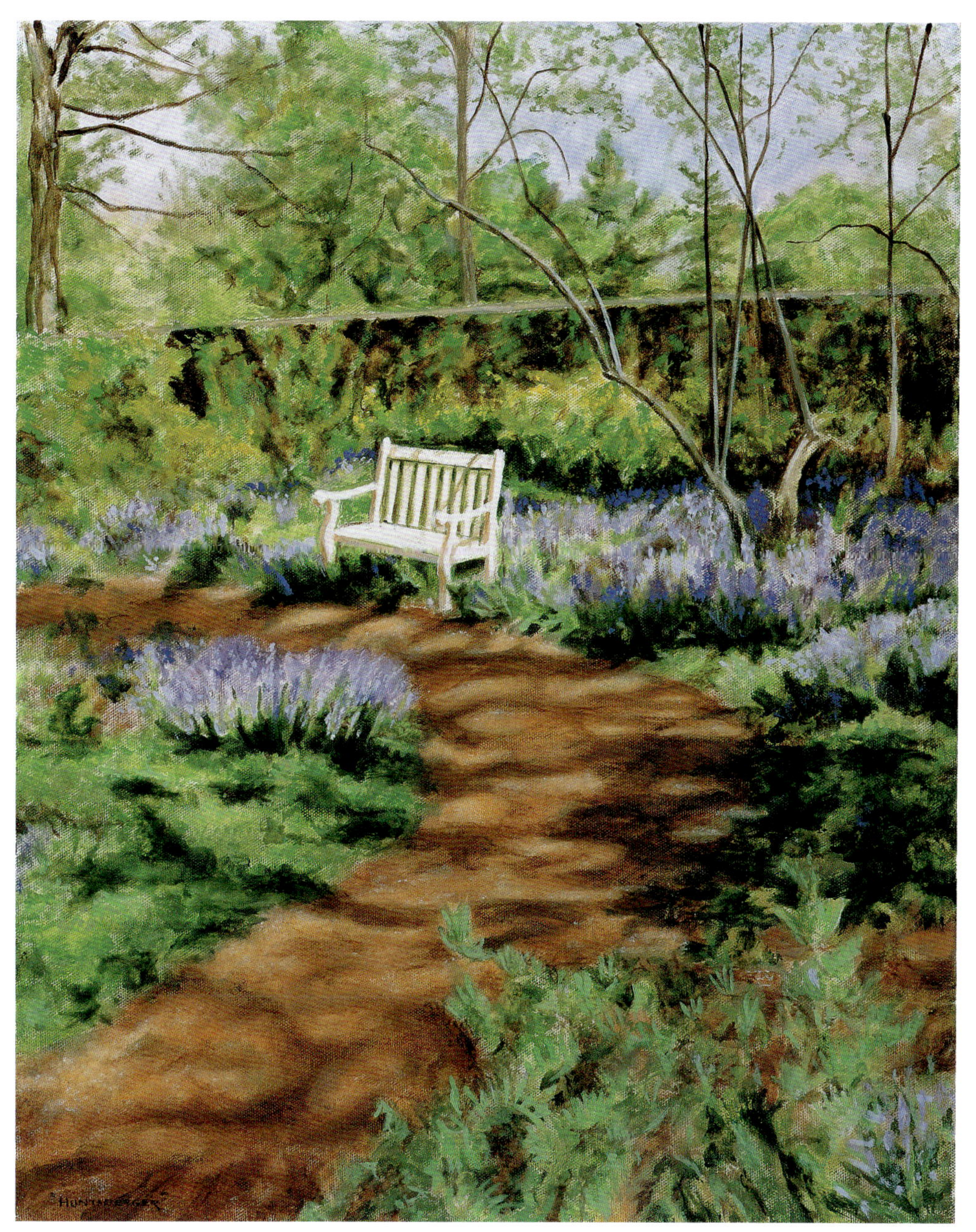

Jessop's Tavern

Built in 1724 by cooper Abraham Jessop, this building at 114 Delaware Street in New Castle, Delaware, has a rich history. Mr. Jessop lived in his home for just a few years. It is not known if his cooperage was on this property. During the 1800s the house may have been a private dwelling or more likely a public house like many of its neighbors because it is located in the block between the courthouse and the Delaware River.

During the early 1900s the building became a tavern with wood shavings on the floor—and shuffleboard to amuse the patrons. The first telephone exchange in New Castle was located on the second floor.

When Tika and Dick Day purchased the property in the 1990s, they completely gutted the building and renovated the space to look as if their tavern had opened for business when the place was built in 1724. They cleverly hid all of the modern conveniences so one has the feeling of dining in a truly early American tavern.

We chose early morning to visit Battery Park in New Castle, Delaware, in order to prospect for scenes that might make attractive paintings. Fortunately when we walked back into old historic New Castle, the light striking one of our favorite restaurants, Jessop's Tavern, made it an obvious choice.

16" x 20" Oil on canvas 1999

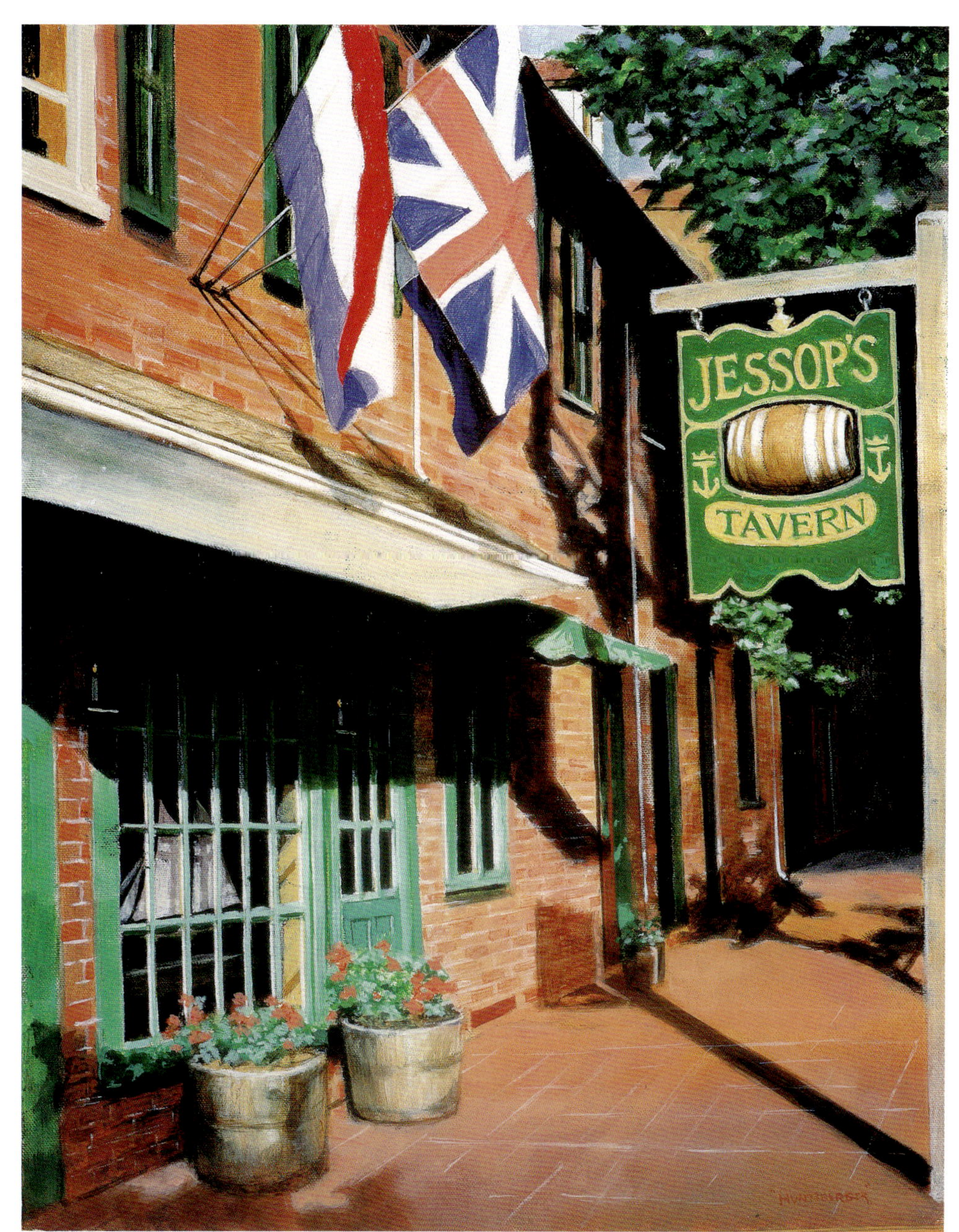
JESSOP'S
TAVERN

Schooner

For many years this schooner held a prominent spot in the lobby of the David Finney Inn in New Castle, Delaware. When the inn burned in 1994, the owner was able to salvage a few things, which he consigned to antique shops in New Hope, Pennsylvania.

One day Tika and Dick Day were visiting New Hope and found the schooner. They purchased the ship to bring it home to New Castle, where it sits in the front window of their Jessop's Tavern, which is just down the street from the old David Finney Inn.

Since childhood I have admired ship models. This one in the window of Jessop's Tavern struck me as an interesting way to depict a model—in the window of a colonial building.

20" x 16" Oil on canvas 1999 Private Collection

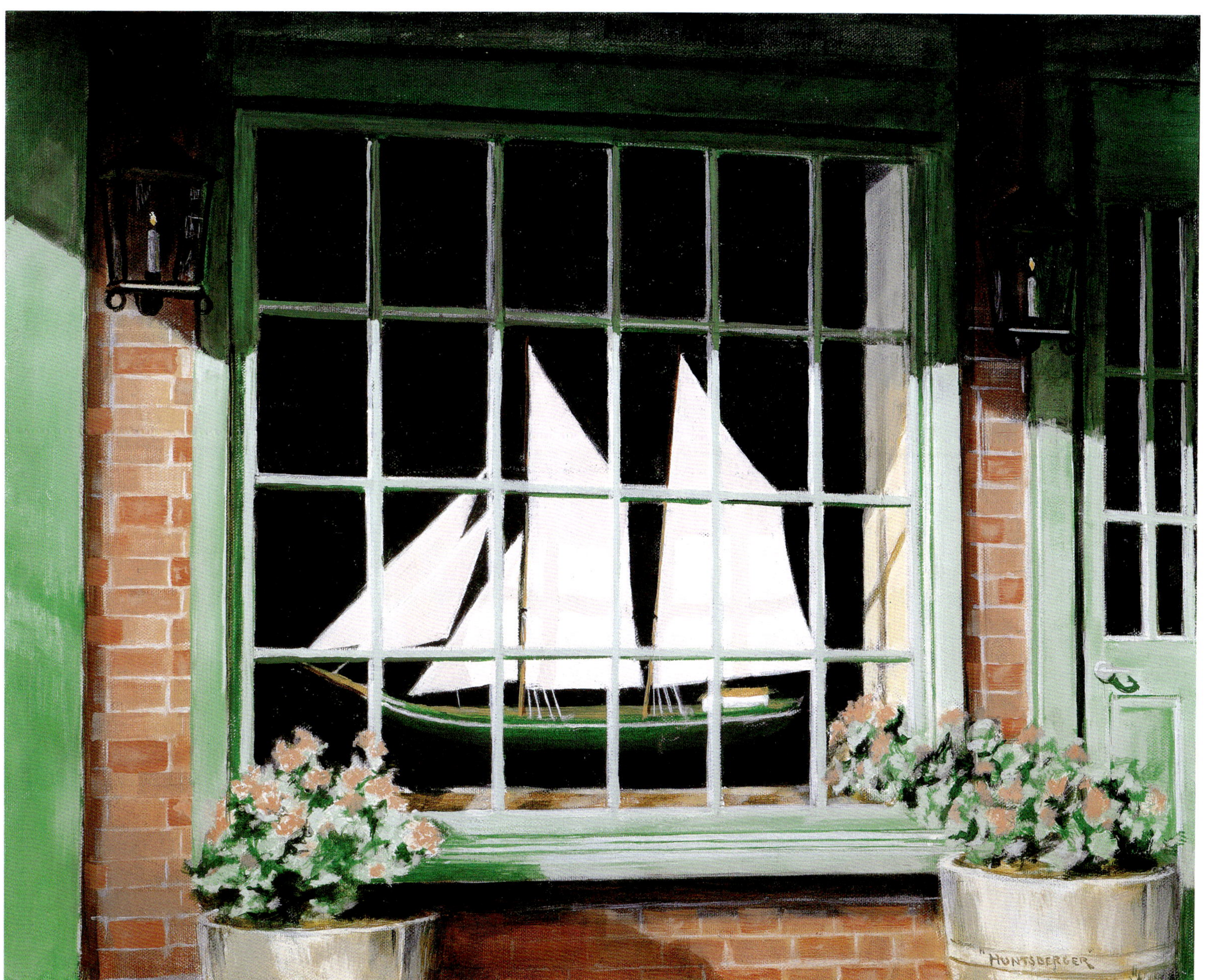
"HUNTSBERGER"

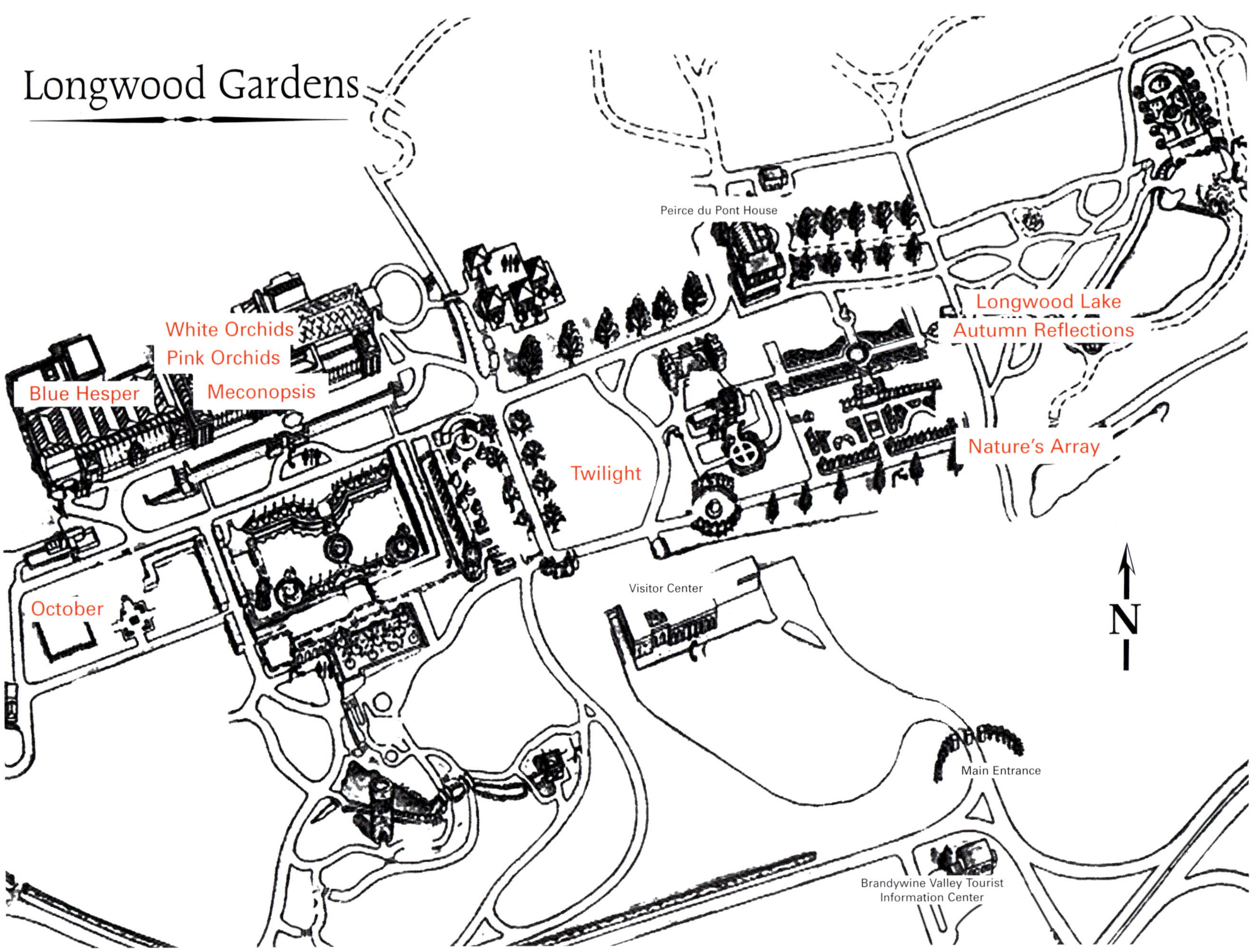
Longwood Gardens
Peirce du Pont House
White Orchids
Pink Orchids
Blue Hesper
Meconopsis
Longwood Lake
Autumn Reflections
Nature's Array
Twilight
Visitor Center
October
N
Main Entrance
Brandywine Valley Tourist
Information Center

CHAPTER FOUR

Longwood Gardens

The Peirce family purchased property near Kennett Square, Pennsylvania, from William Penn in 1700. Joshua and Samuel Peirce established an arboretum on the family farm in 1798. By 1850 Peirce's Park was recognized as one of the finest collections of trees in the nation. In 1906 Pierre S. du Pont (1870-1954), a great-grandson of DuPont Company founder E. I. du Pont, purchased the farm to preserve the trees, which were in danger of being logged for timber. He created Longwood Gardens at Peirce's Park.

The du Pont family has a long tradition of gardening, and Pierre was one of its greatest gardeners. At first he operated under no master plan as he built the gardens bit by bit. Planting flower walks and shrubs, he erected rose-laden trellises and built many fountains and pools.

Although Pierre enlarged the Peirce House by connecting the old and new wings with a lavishly planted conservatory and making it very comfortable, this was not as grand a home as one might expect a person of his wealth to inhabit.

After visiting the Villa Gori in Siena, Italy, Pierre was inspired to build an open air theatre on the site of the original Peirce barn. Opened in June 1914, the theatre boasts 750 illuminated water jets to serve as both the stage "curtain" and post-performance display.

In 1914 Pierre formed Longwood, Inc., to maintain the gardens in perpetuity. Without children, he concentrated on Longwood's future and clearly considered the gardens part of the du Pont family legacy to the greater community. Thanks to his farsightedness, generosity, and insistence on professional management, these gardens continue to grow and prosper long after his death in 1954.

Longwood Lake

The Large Lake often appears a dazzling green. The iron-topped gazebo, a favorite spot for taking family photographs, is one of three on the property.

Beyond the weeping willow *(Salix babylonica)* at the far end of the Large Lake is a terrace that overlooks the formal Italian water garden.

This has always been my favorite among the many beautiful sites at Longwood Gardens. The willow in the background is gone now.

20" x 16" Oil on canvas 1994 Private Collection

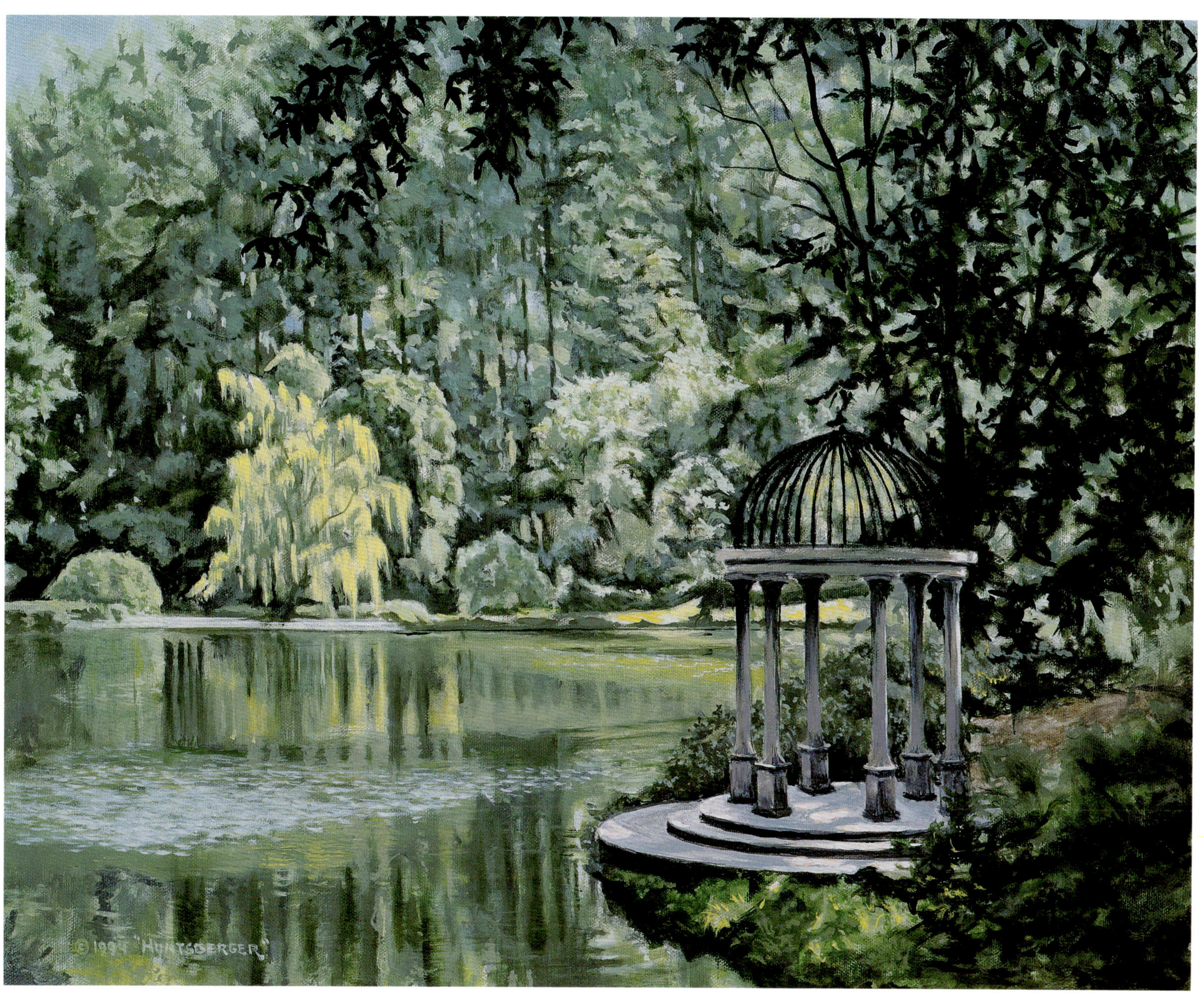
HUNTSBERGER

Autumn Reflections

During autumn the reflections of colorful leaves and berries on the rippling water surface of the Large Lake give an abstract appearance to a natural scene. This was the view across the lake from a spot near the gazebo.

Visiting this Longwood lake in autumn, I was struck by the colorful reflections on the water. I decided to do a semiabstract by painting only the reflections.

14" x 11" Oil on canvas 1992 Collection of Warren B. Burt

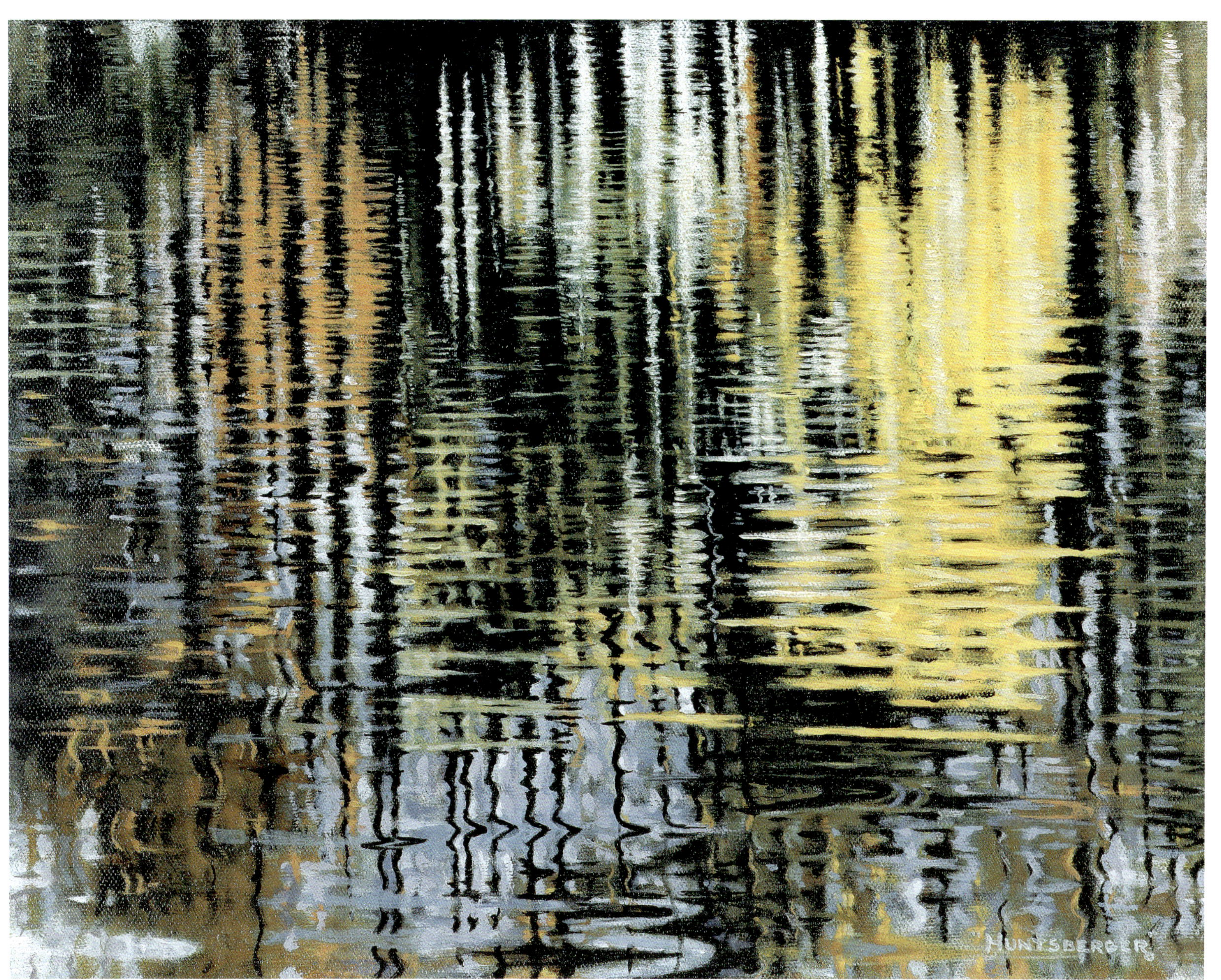
HUNTSBERGER

Nature's Array

Bald Cypress (Taxodium distichum) trees grow on the edge of the Small Lake at Longwood Gardens. A little garden arrangement established itself in one of the stumps, and it changes with the seasons. The little clump of vegetation seemed to comprise an arrangement when viewed at the proper angle. I could not resist painting it.

14" x 18" Oil on canvas 1995 Eric & Jane Patrick Casey

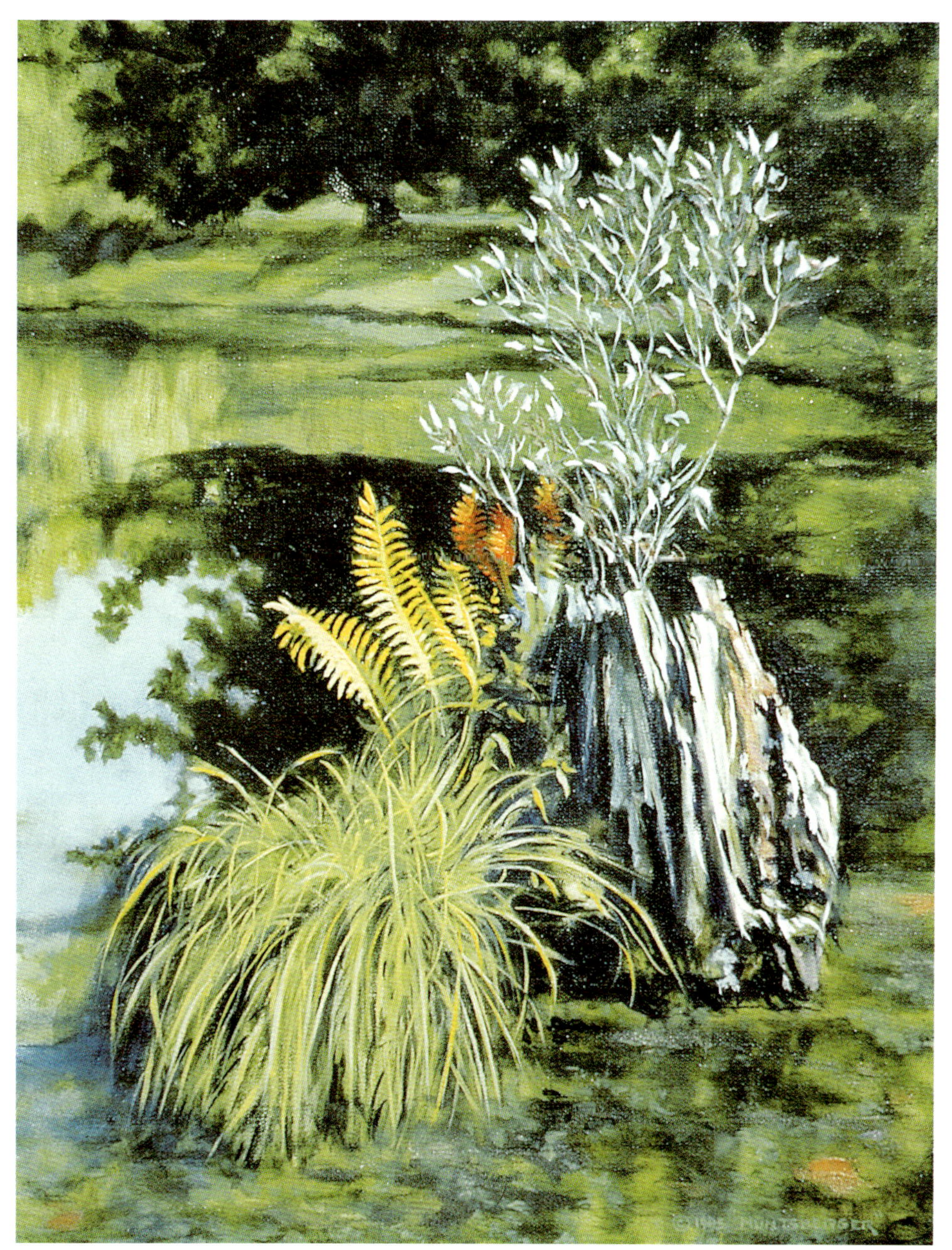

Blue Hesper

Longwood Gardens, the horticultural showplace near Kennett Square, Pennsylvania, exhibits plants in garden settings. This aesthetic goal is emphasized— rather than simply enlarging the variety of plants in the collections that already contain more than two hundred different plant families.

Pierre S. du Pont opened his massive conservatory in 1921 to provide a setting for the indoor display of plants that do not thrive in Pennsylvania's climate and to enjoy sophisticated flower garden displays out of season. Over the years the attached greenhouses were expanded and improved, and additional exhibition spaces were built. In 1966 a huge Palm House opened.

The opulent Longwood conservatories include approximately sixty species and varieties of palms among their plantings. This Blue Hesper Palm *(Brahea armata)* is among the showiest specimens found in the Palm House.

I had painted a clump of Agave, which I saw in California, and was pleased with the results. When I saw the blue hesper, I wanted to paint it in a similar fashion.

36" x 36" Oil on canvas 1997

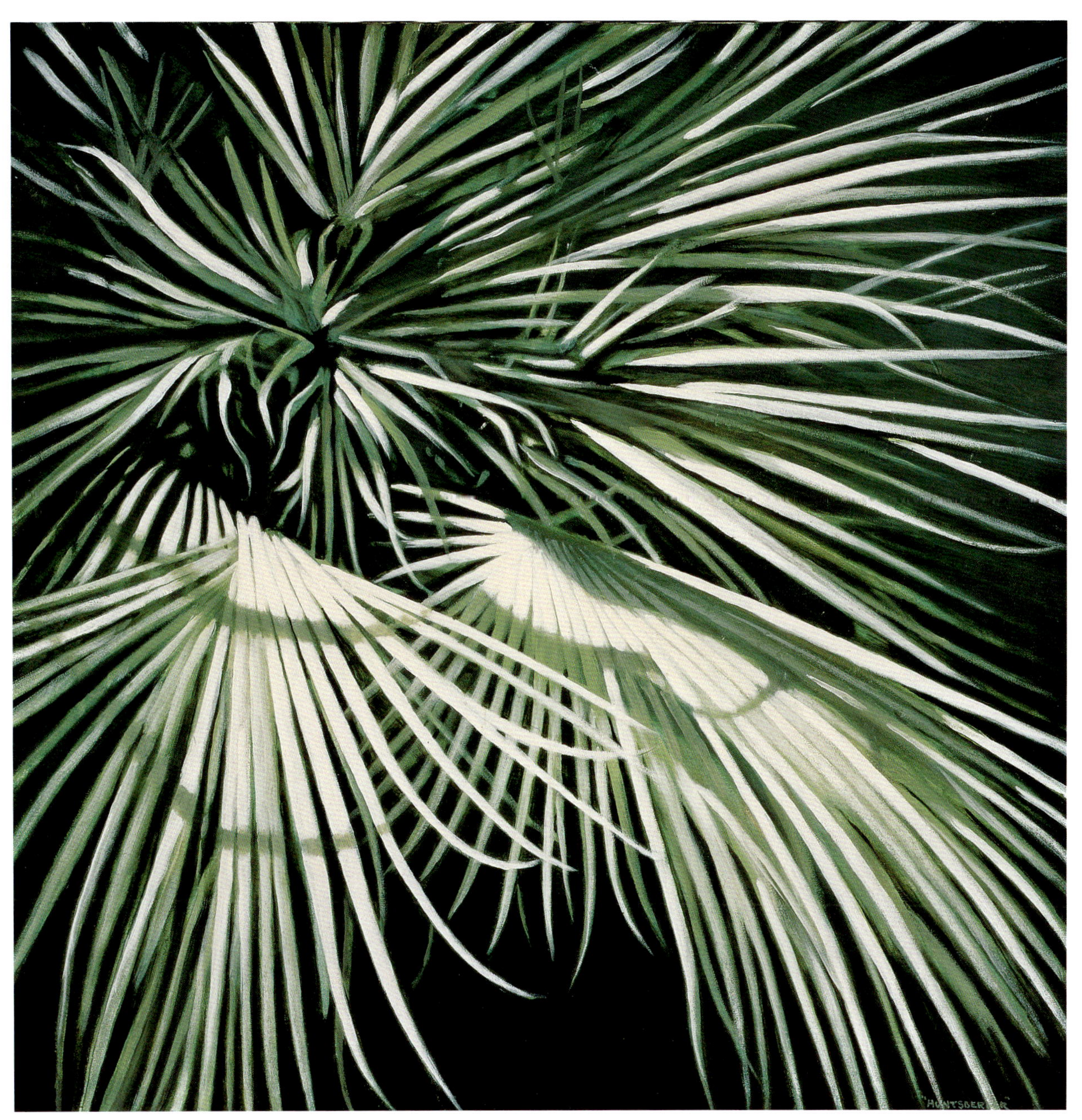

White Orchids

The Longwood plant collection, begun by Pierre S. du Pont, now contains more that 3,200 types of orchid. To provide continuous bloom, color, and scent, the gardeners choose two to five hundred of these specimens for public display from the 7,500 orchid plants growing in Longwood's five orchid-growing houses.

I was very pleased to receive so many compliments rom artist colleagues about this little painting.

12" x 16" Oil on canvas 2002 Collection of Mrs. David Craven

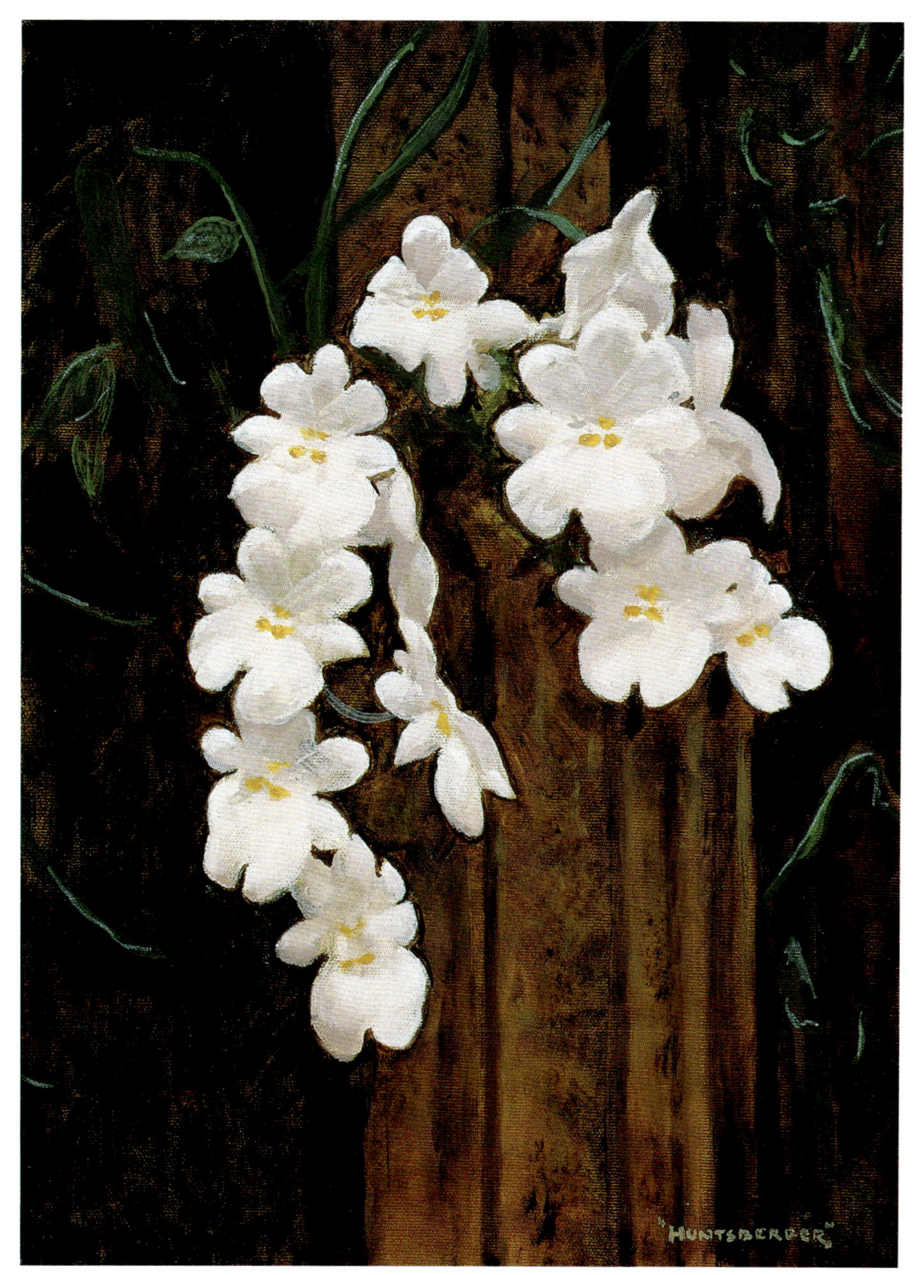
"HUNTSBERGER"

Pink Orchids

The orchids in the Longwood Conservatory are arranged against a background of ivy and other green foliage plants. I thoroughly enjoyed painting these lovely orchids. I was pleased when this painting was accepted in the Havre de Grace (Maryland) Arts Commission National Juried Show for 2003

24" x 24" Oil on canvas 2003 Collection of Mrs. David Craven

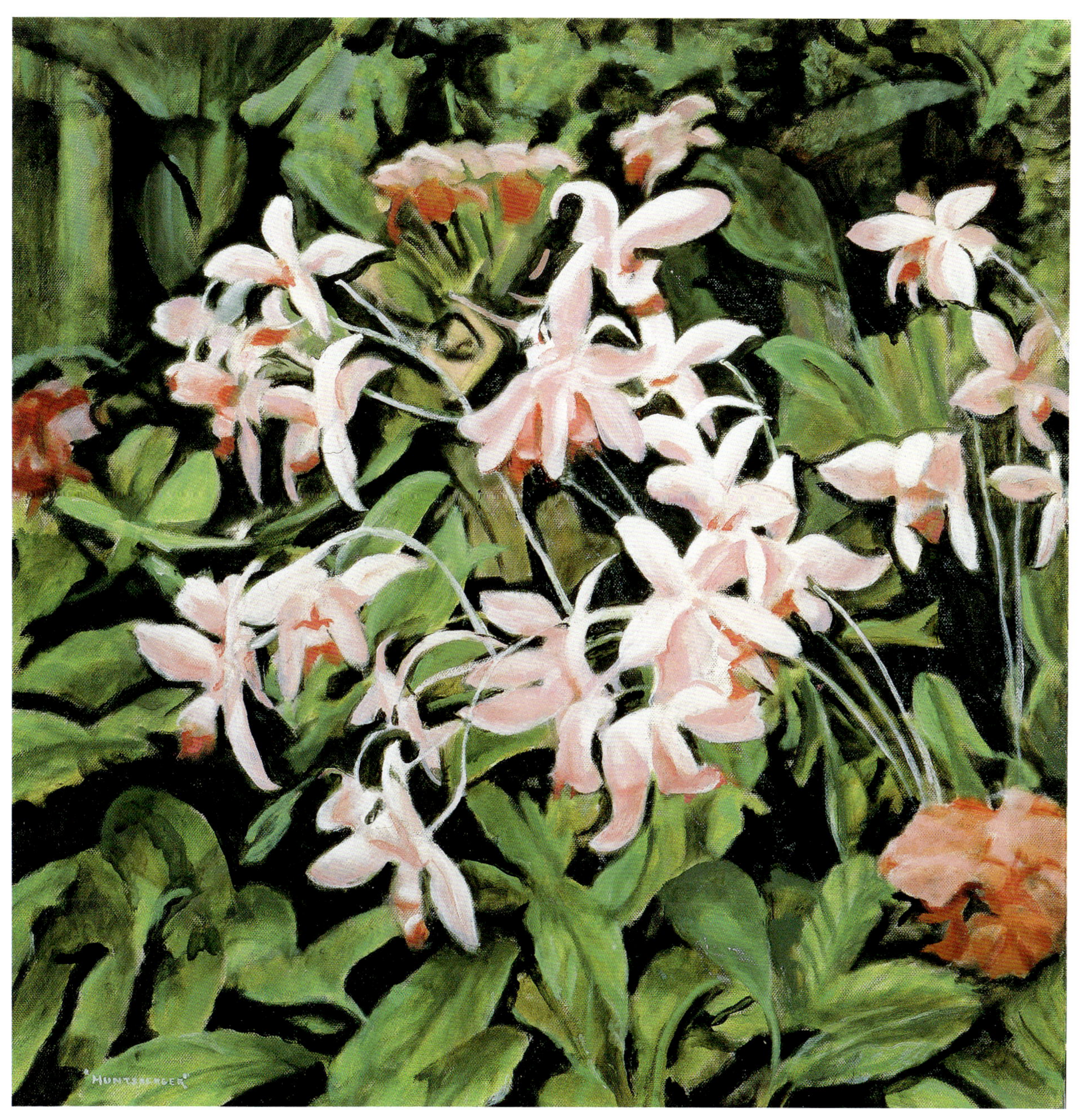

Meconopsis

The Longwood staff carefully cultivates these rare blue poppies in the greenhouse because the blossoms wouldn't survive the sultry summers of the Brandywine Valley. The poppies bloom freely in Scotland, Alaska and the Himalayas where summers are cool.

The Blue Poppy Nursery in Alaska ships the plants to Longwood during October. The state-of-the-art technology in Longwood greenhouse allows the staff to mimic ideal environmental conditions. The plants bloom in early March and are placed in large masses for display in the Conservatory.

I found these blue poppies in the Longwood conservatory in March 2003. The large flowers were held aloft on slender stems above the foliage. The soft blue was luminous in the early afternoon sunlight that shone through the conservatory windows. I forgot the snow and ice outside and enjoyed an early taste of summer.

11" x 14" Oil on canvas 2003 Collection of Mrs. David Craven

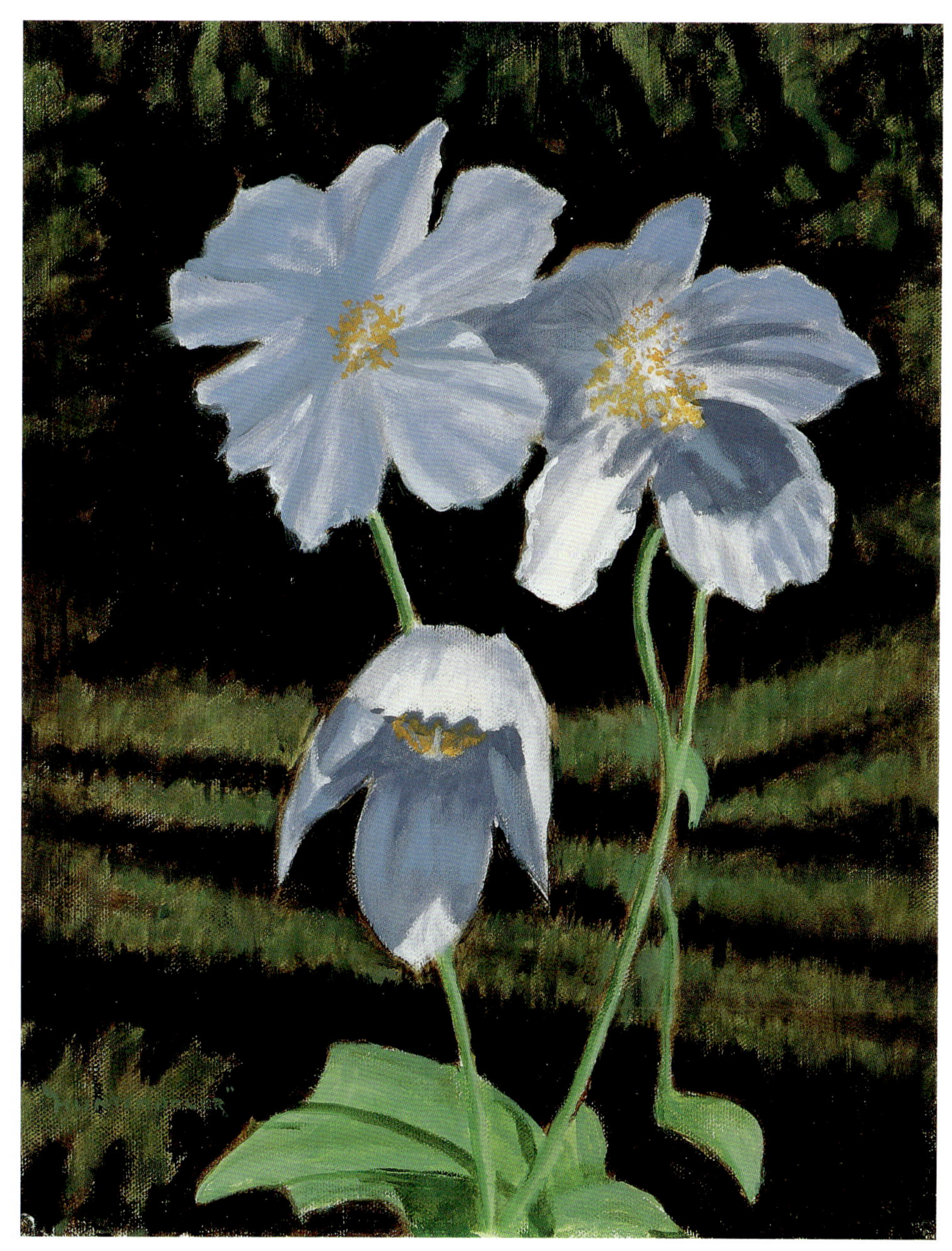

October

In 1973 a team of landscape architects and Longwood gardeners started to build the outdoor Idea Garden at Longwood. This garden is refurbished often and educates visitors about the latest in annuals, perennials, ground covers, vines, berries, herbs, fruit trees, grasses, roses, and vegetables that grow well in the Brandywine Valley.

Many visitors continue to garner ideas from the well-labeled displays and may take home information sheets, which are housed in convenient mailboxes set up throughout the Idea Garden.

During October we visited the Idea Garden and were delighted to find these pumpkins and corn shocks arranged as if in a scene from our childhood. It evoked memories of my dad's favorite James Whitcomb Riley poem, which I often recited to my own children. "When the frost is on the pumpkin and the fodder's in the shock…."

16" x 12" Oil on canvas 1989 Collection of Mr. & Mrs. Tom Newnam

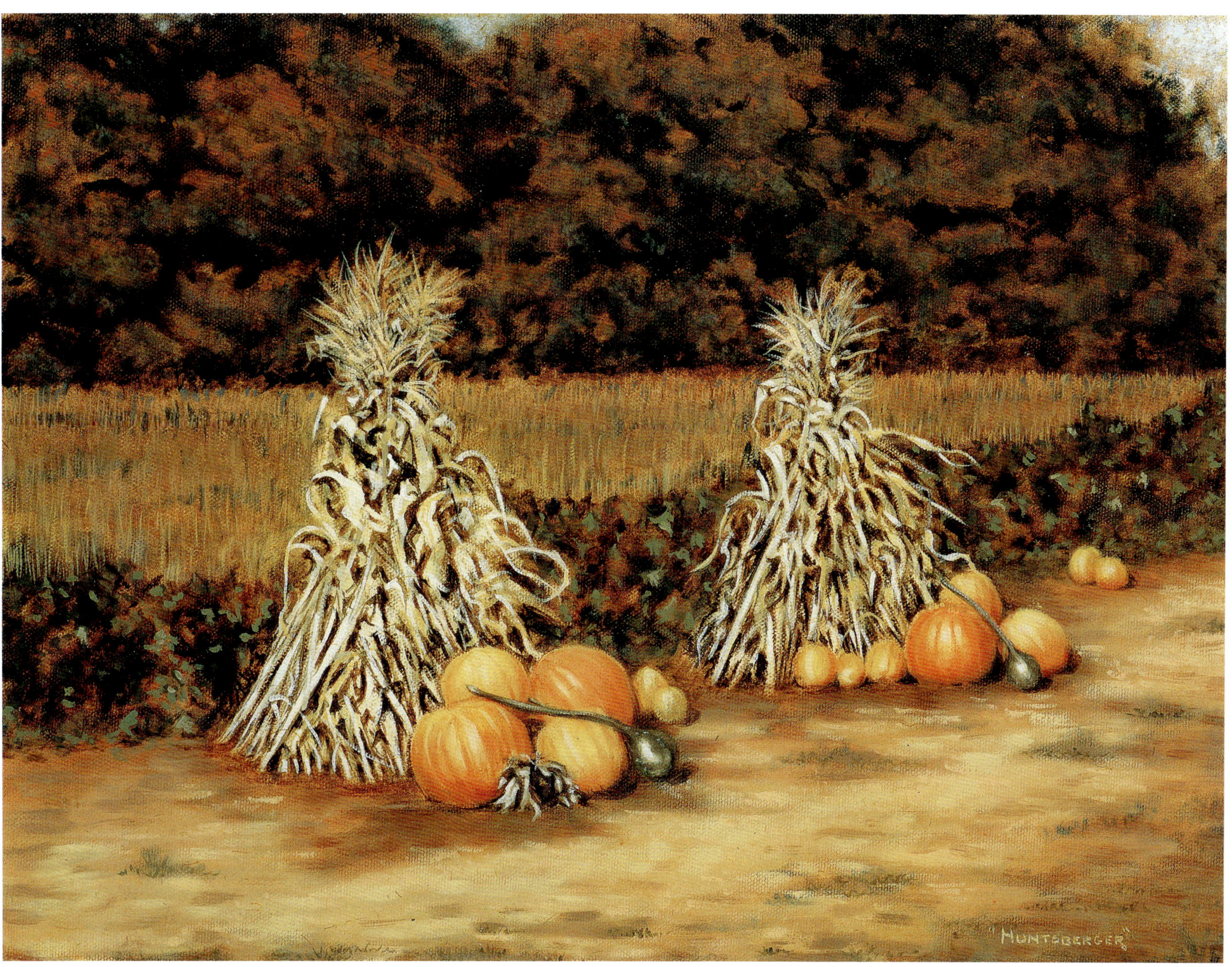
"HUNTSBERGER"

Twilight

At Longwood Gardens, an allée of Princess Trees *(Paulownia tomentosa)* lined one of the walks from the visitor center to the conservatory. During May the trees were covered with massive lavender blossoms before the large leaves appeared, and during the winter, the tortured limbs made interesting designs against the sky.

The huge trees pictured here were replaced with young saplings in 2001. Paulownias grow so quickly that it will only be a few years before the allée is restored to grandeur.

This is a twilight view during December while Janet and I were waiting for Longwood's famous Christmas light display to be illuminated. A few moments after we had seen these marvelous colors, the sky became completely dark. I didn't know then that these beautiful trees would soon disappear, so I am especially pleased to have painted them before their demise.

20" x 16" Oil on canvas 2000 Private Collection

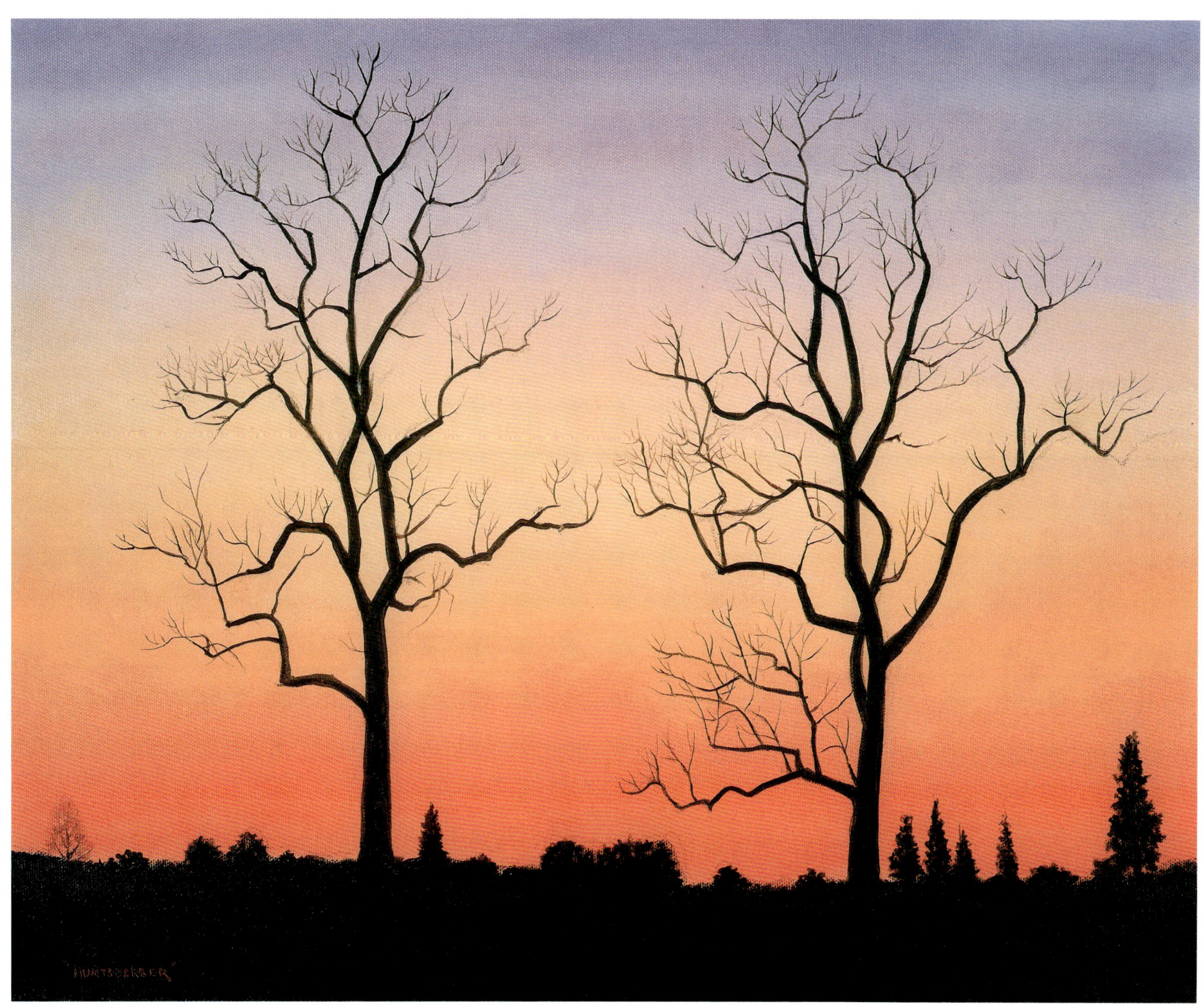
HUNTSBERGER

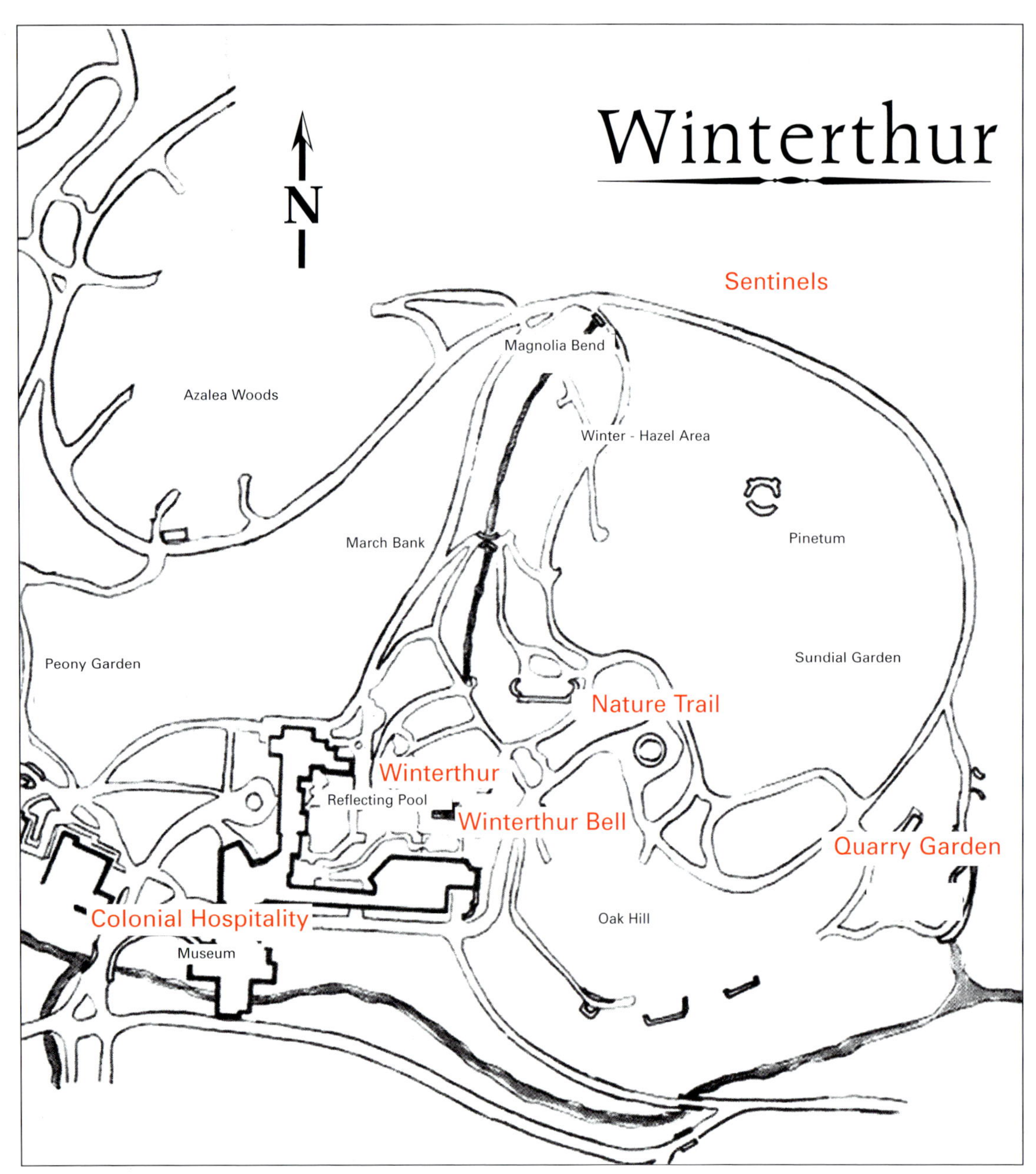
Winterthur
N
Sentinels
Magnolia Bend
Azalea Woods
Winter - Hazel Area
Pinetum
March Bank
Sundial Garden
Peony Garden
Nature Trail
Winterthur
Reflecting Pool
Winterthur Bell
Quarry Garden
Colonial Hospitality
Oak Hill
Museum

Chapter Five

Winterthur

Seven miles west of Wilmington a long winding driveway from Kennett Pike leads to the Winterthur Museum and Gardens. Evelina du Pont Bidermann and her husband, Jacques Antoine, built the earliest part of the masonry and cream-colored stucco home in 1838. Later the mansion was greatly expanded by their great-nephew, Henry F. du Pont, who collected high-quality American furniture and artifacts during the early twentieth century at a time when other wealthy Americans were buying European antiques.

Henry F. du Pont purchased architectural elements of fine early American houses to become the interiors of his museum rooms. He acquired the façades of colonial buildings before they were destroyed and rebuilt them to form a colonial-style courtyard within the museum. He filled Winterthur with his collections of rare antiques, paintings, and household furnishings. At auctions he often bid against private collectors and buyers from other American museums. His collections of furniture, ceramics, textiles, base metals, and early American silver (which include tankards made by Paul Revere) are world renowned.

Within the grand old trees surrounding his mansion, Mr. du Pont planned a garden that reaches its peak in spring and autumn, the seasons he was in residence. He swapped plants with the foremost horticulturists of his day to fill his gardens with many rare and unusual specimens. When the chestnut blight cut wide swathes through his forest, he chose to replace the destroyed trees with azaleas and rhododendrons. These create a glorious spring display, which draws visitors from around the world in early May.

Winterthur has continued to expand. A seamless addition, with arches stretching over a small stream, mimics a French château. An "Enchanted Garden" for children was built where the du Pont children once played.

Winterthur Steps

(Winterthur)

Henry F. du Pont improved the landscape areas adjacent to his residence assisted by Marian Cruger Coffin's designs for the Sundial Garden, the Peony Garden, and the terraced gardens leading to the Reflecting Pool. Winterthur offers many handsome façades. This one with the columned porch and the steps leading to the Reflecting Pool has always struck me as one of the most attractive. Before the deciduous trees have leafed, a slightly raised area above the pool provides this scene.

16" x 20" Oil on canvas 2002 Collection of Mr. & Mrs. David Brennen

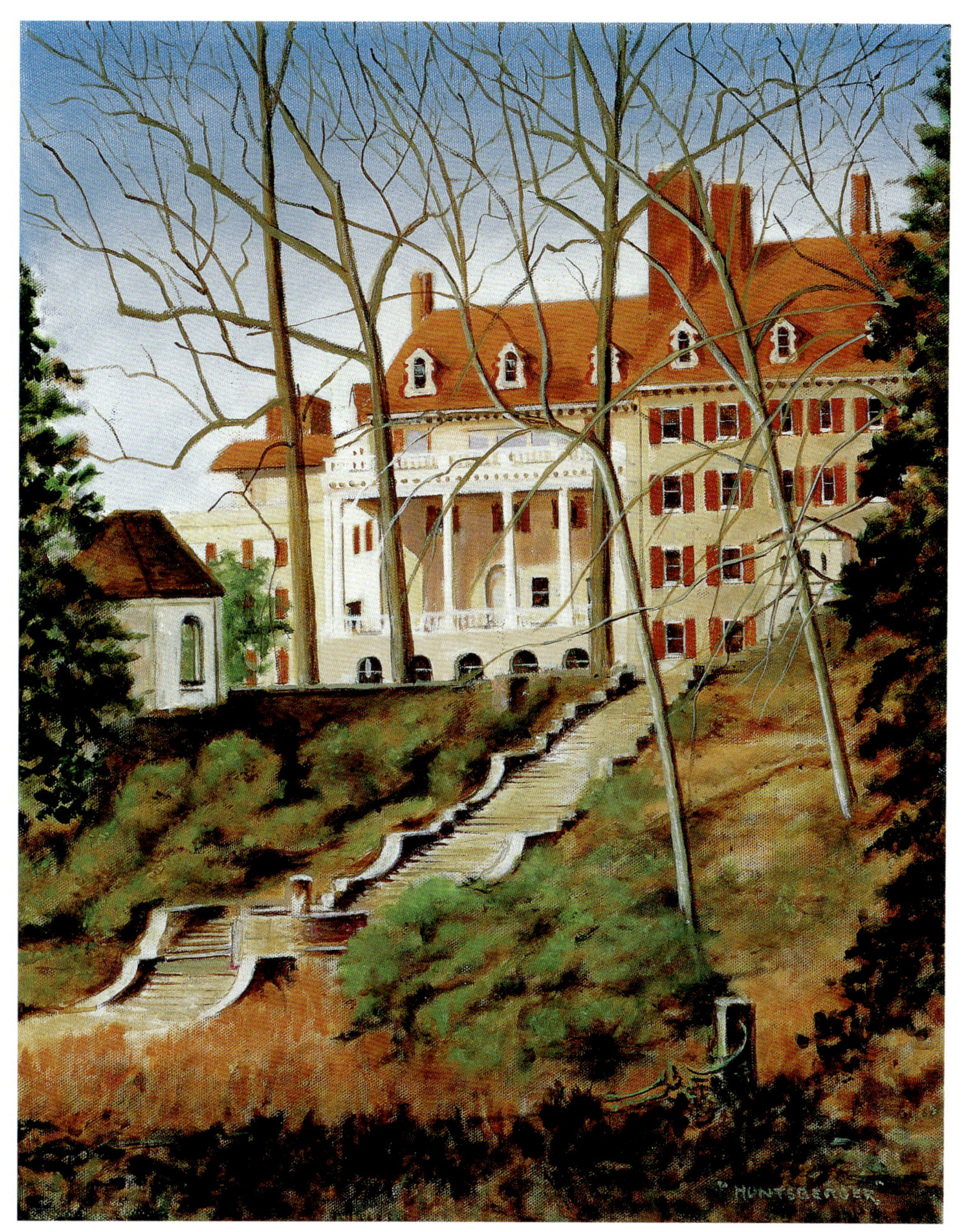
"HUNTSBERGER"

Winterthur Bell

Two stone pool houses stand at the east end of the intimate Reflecting Pool area. Their architecture echoes that of the gazebo at the top of the steps to the house. This metal bell is anchored to the wall of one of these houses. When the du Pont family lived at Winterthur, the Reflecting Pool was a swimming pool.

I have walked through Winterthur's grounds during all seasons and times of day. Consequently, I was shocked to see this bell for the first time not long ago. I must have passed by countless times without noticing it. With the morning sunlight striking the bell and casting a beautiful shadow, it suddenly commanded my full attention. I knew I must paint this.

12" x 16" Oil on canvas 2002 Collection of Mr. & Mrs. Allan R. Dever

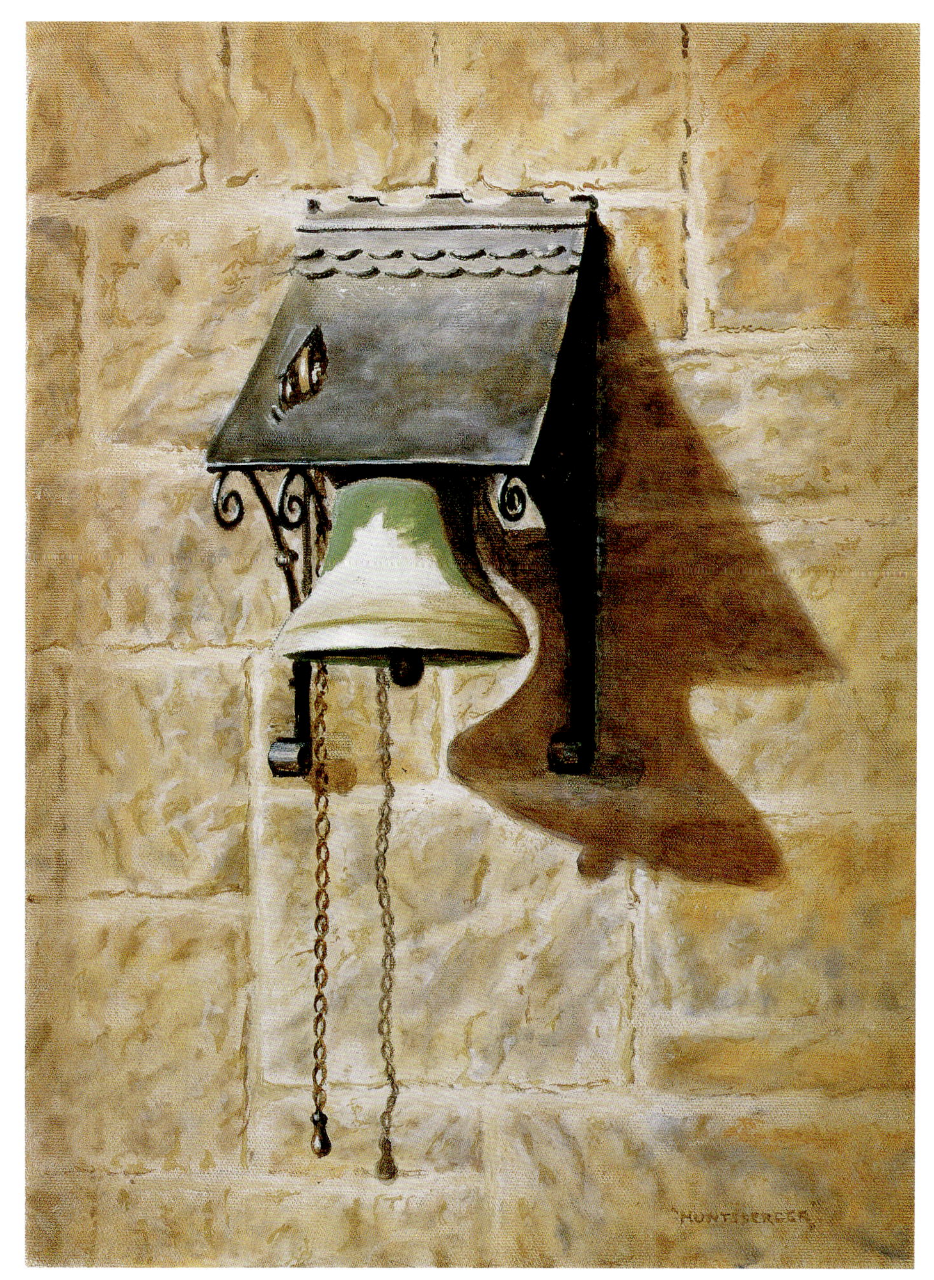
HUNTSBERGER

Nature Trail

One of the very desirable aspects of the Winterthur gardens is the endless variety of vistas one encounters. This fall scene with the strong backlighting was quite appealing to me.

20" x 16" Oil on canvas 1990 Corporate Collection

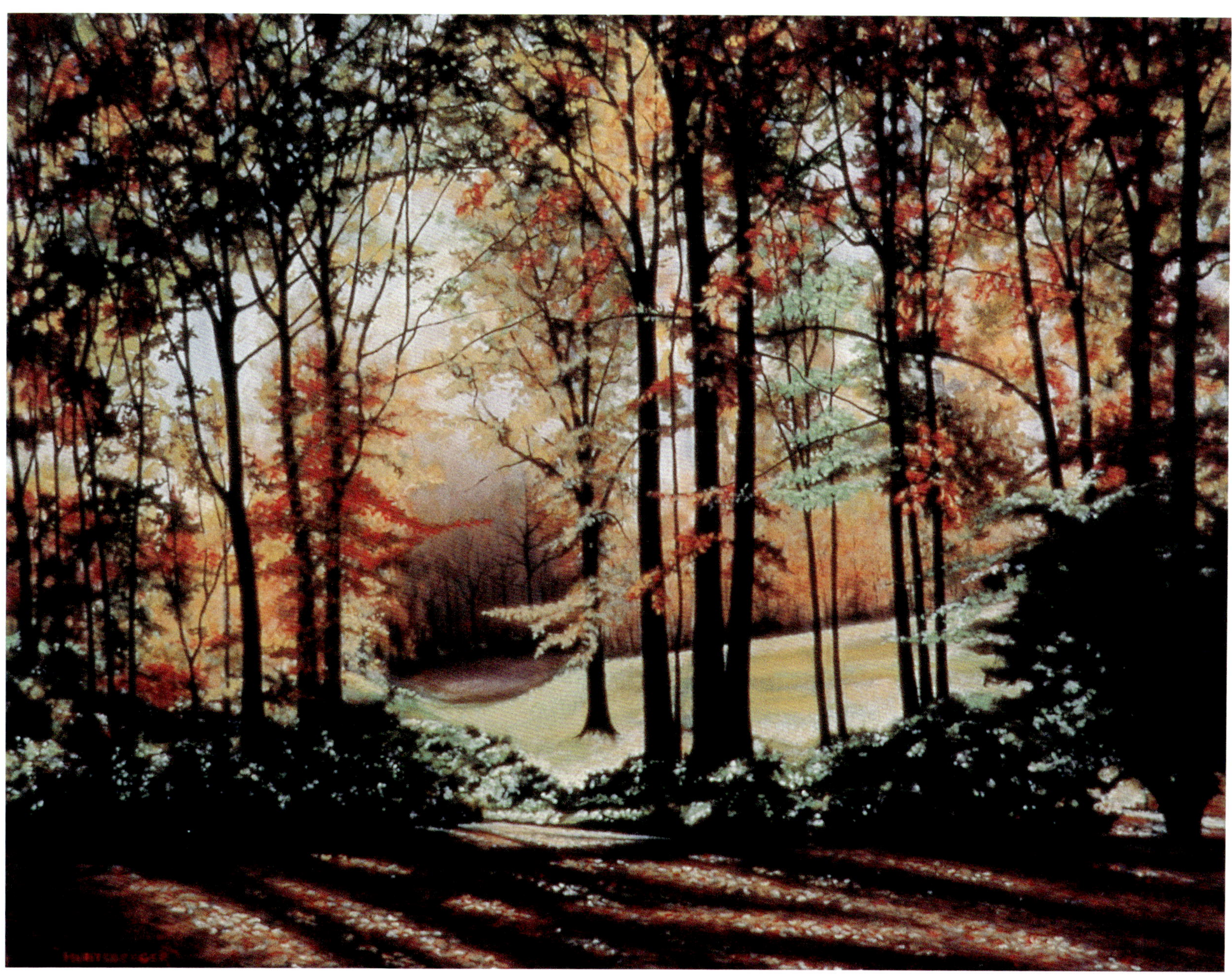

The Quarry Garden

Henry F. du Pont was eighty-two years old in 1962 when he undertook his last garden creation. He supervised the transformation of an old stone quarry into a spectacular garden. Natural springs provide enough water to sustain the oriental candelabra primulas and other plants that thrive in boggy soil.

The densely planted primulas provide marvelous color when they bloom. Ferns, perennials, and shrubs fill niches in the rock outcroppings that form the quarry walls. Late blooming azaleas enhance the slopes adjacent to the quarry.

The graceful sweep of the walk and patio overlooking the quarry garden has always been among my favorite areas of Winterthur.

20" x 16" Oil on canvas 1988

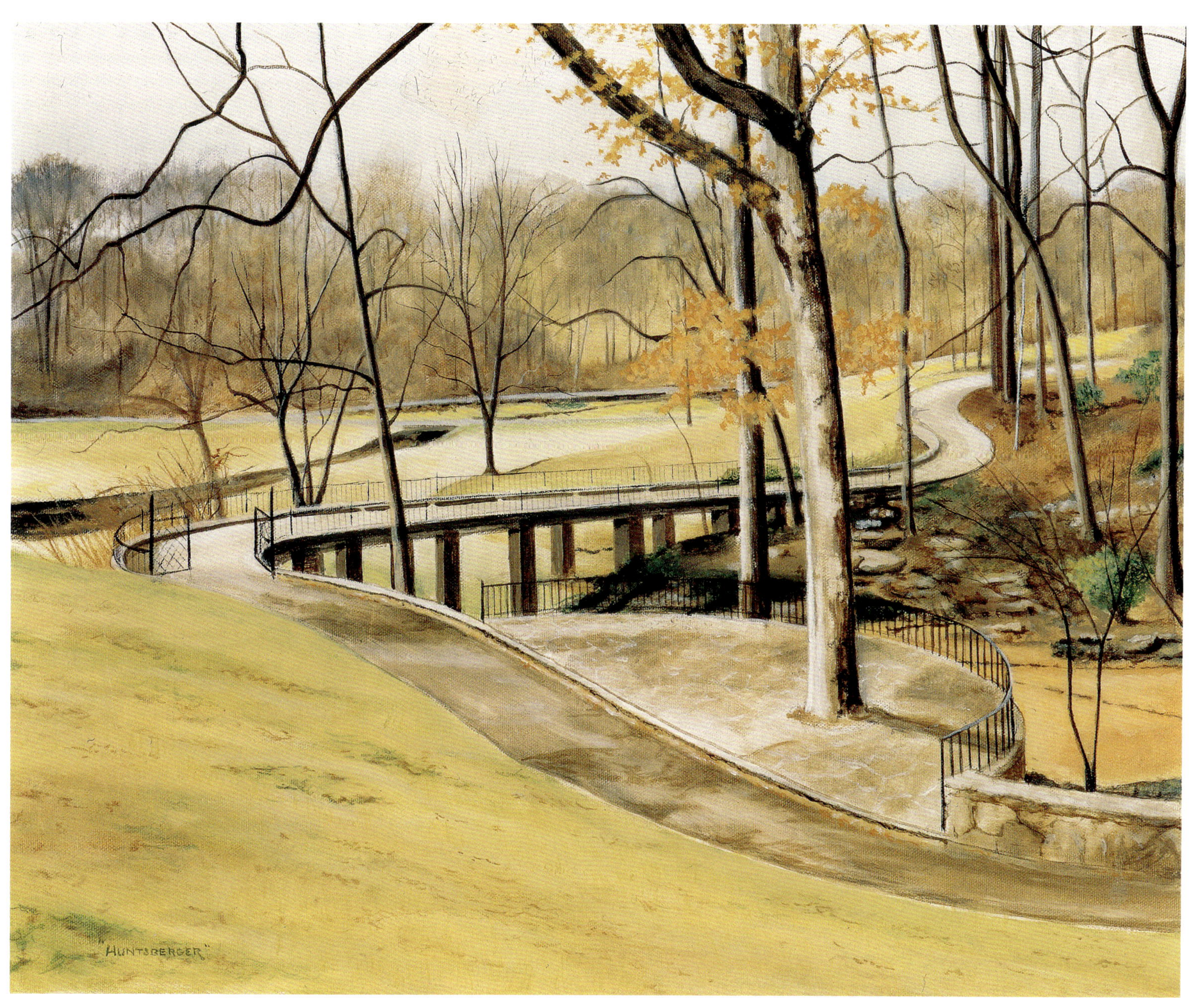
"HUNTSBERGER"

The Sentinels

These eighty-year-old specimen sargent cherry trees (Prunus sargentii) stand near Winterthur's Garden Lane on the edge of a major green space, the Greensward. In winter the trees display their well-tended shape; in spring their branches have pink buds and creamy white flowers.

Across the Garden Lane the pink colors of the Korean rhododendron blend well with the cherry blossoms and stand out sharply against the dark green evergreen trees in the nearby Pinetum.

These two cherry trees stand alone and apart from the others, which are on the opposite side of the road. They seem to command and stand guard over the terrain beyond. They are a delight in all seasons, but I find their leafless time best.

24" x 18" Oil on canvas 1989 Collection of Virginia A. Harris

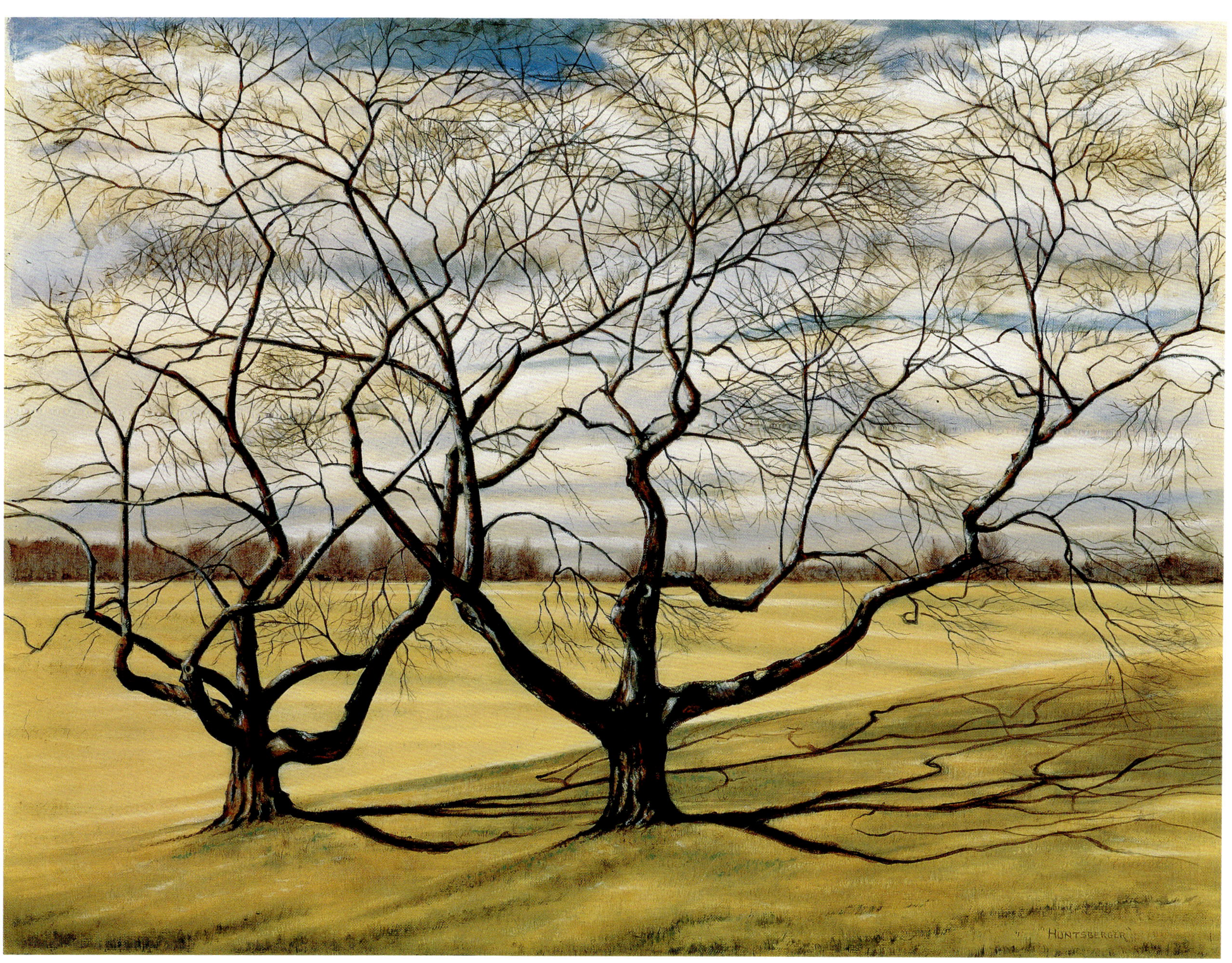
HUNTSBERGER

Colonial Hospitality

This beautiful still was part of an exhibit at Winterthur Museum. When I inquired why it was included in a display of early American home furnishings, I was told that guests arriving at the homes of wealthy colonials would expect to be served spirits for refreshment. Therefore, one would expect to find a still on the premises of early American stately homes. I had never seen a still like this and thought it would make a colorful painting. The owner of this painting purchased it at a Ronald McDonald House benefit. She was staying at the "Ronald" in Wilmington, Delaware, while her son was receiving treatment at the renowned Alfred I. du Pont Hospital for Children.

18" x 18" Oil on canvas 1997 Collection of Yoshiko Aoki

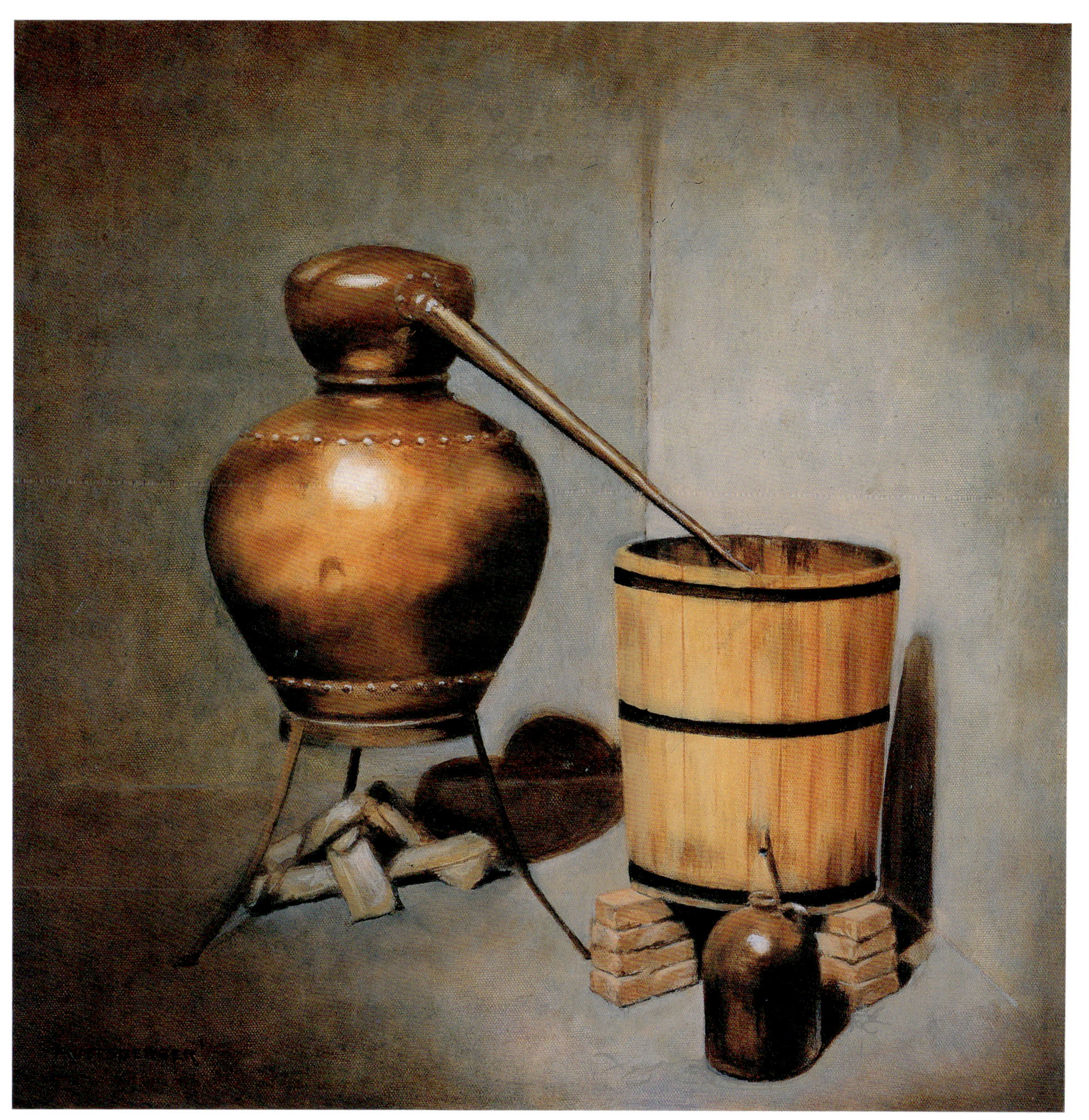

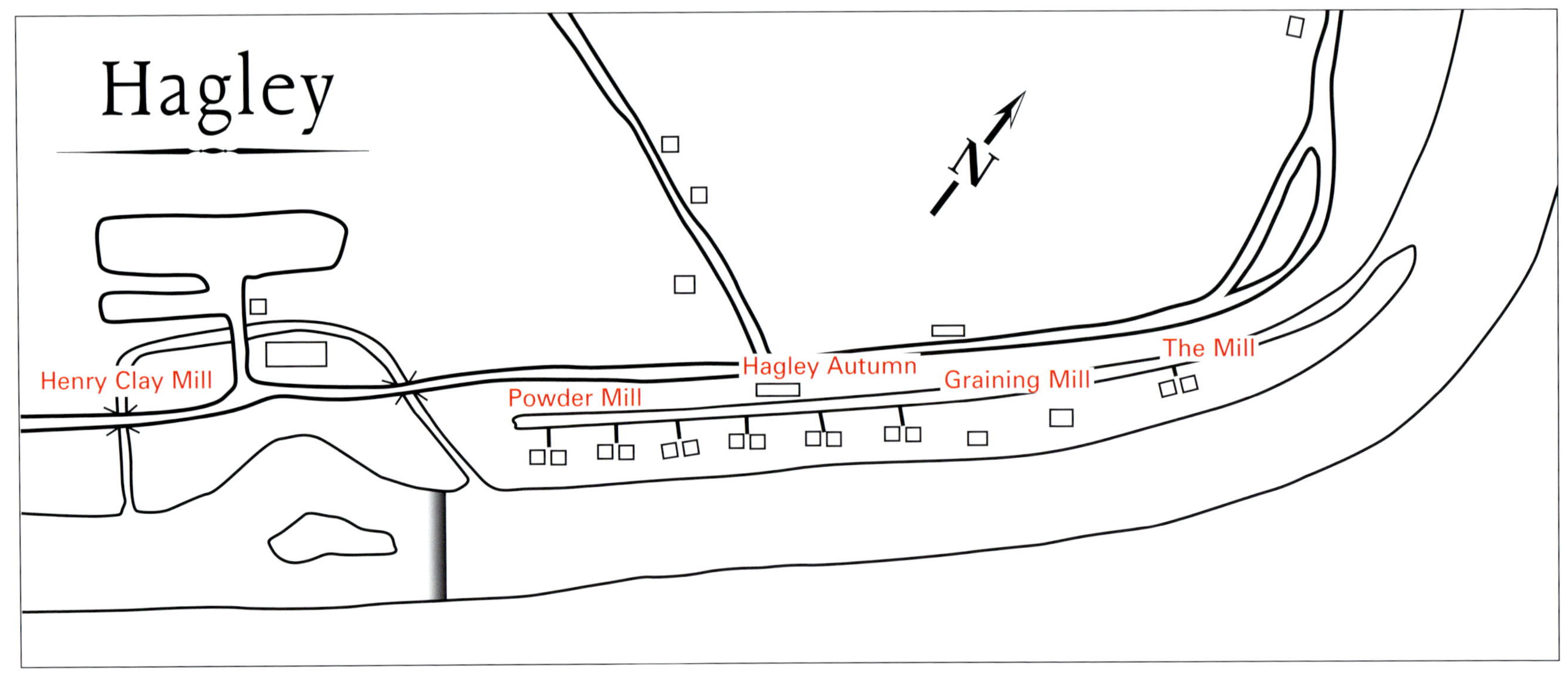
Hagley
N
Henry Clay Mill
Powder Mill
Hagley Autumn
Graining Mill
The Mill

Chapter Six

Hagley

The Hagley Foundation owns and maintains the grounds and mills along the Brandywine River in Wilmington, Delaware, where the du Pont family manufactured black powder. This mill site was chosen because the river current was strong enough to produce power and the riverbanks were covered with willow trees for making charcoal. Black powder was produced here from 1803 to 1921.

Eleutherian Mills, the du Pont family ancestral home, is located on the Hagley property. Built in 1802-3, this charming Georgian-style residence contains antiques and possessions belonging to five generations of du Ponts. In 1923 Henry A. du Pont gave the home to his daughter Louise Evelina du Pont Crowninshield with the stipulation that she live in it for part of each year.

Mrs. Crowninshield restored her great-grandparent's house, lived in it each year during May and October, and finally gave her family's home and dormant powder mills to the Hagley Foundation. She and her brother Henry F. du Pont (of Winterthur) made outstanding contributions to the world of antiques and historical preservation.

In 1953 the Hagley Foundation began the restoration of the grounds and buildings to transform a 160-acre area into a beautiful historical center. Winding roads and footpaths connect the buildings in this beautiful river valley.

Hagley Autumn

Fall has always been my favorite season. This colorful view looks South from the road along the Brandywine, which leads from the original du Pont home and the Elutherian Mills to Hagley and the Henry Clay Mill. Continuing past the gate, the road passes Breck's Mill, then Walker's Mill, and the DuPont Experimental Station (where I worked for many years) before turning west to meet the Kennett Pike.

20" x 16" Oil on canvas 1996 Collection of Cheryl Cantrell

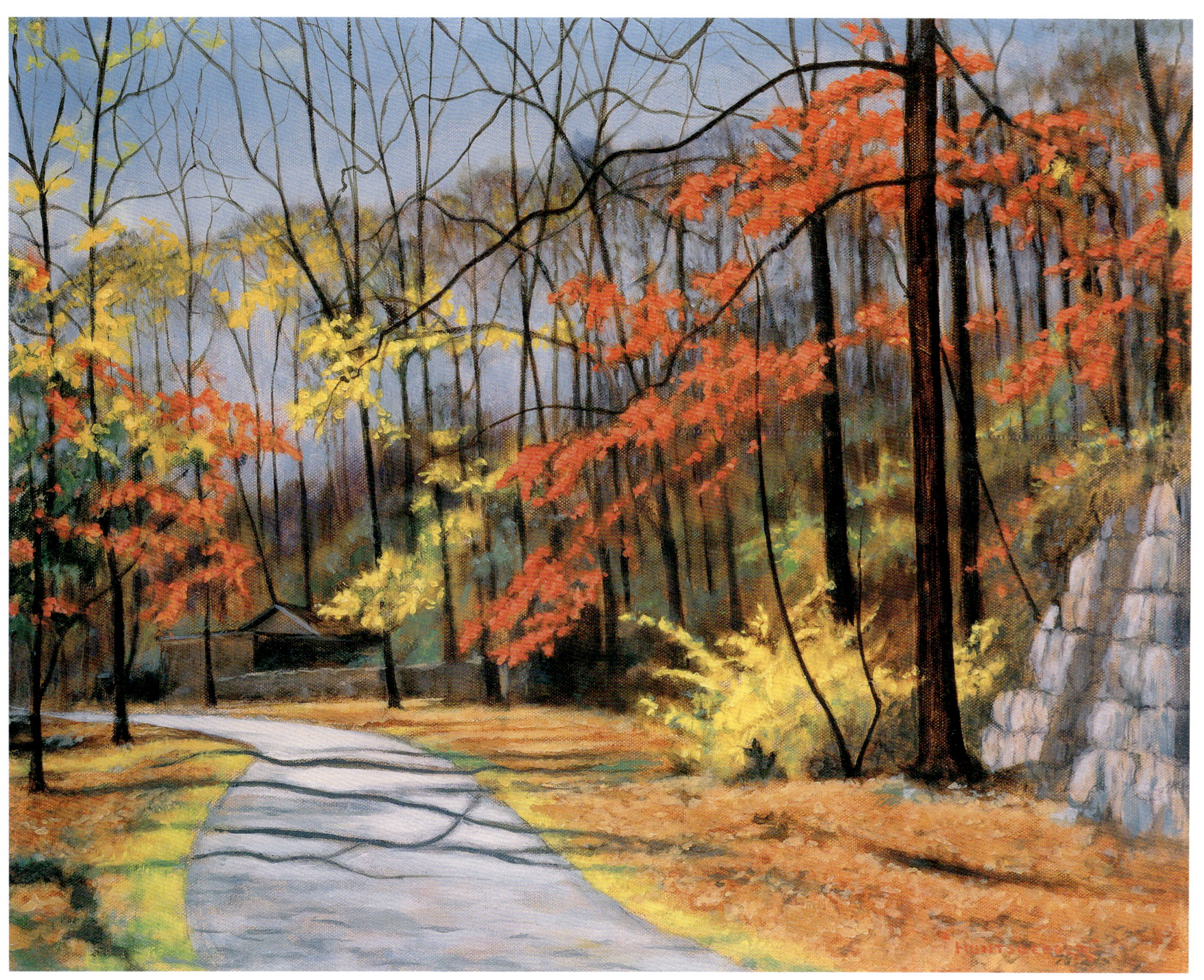

Henry Clay Mill

This handsome stone structure with brick trim, built in 1814 as a textile mill, is the main building of the Hagley Museum. In 1844 it was converted to the Henry Clay Keg Factory for the manufacture and storage of the kegs used for the powder produced in the adjacent DuPont powder yards. The factory was closed in 1921 when the production of powder was halted.

After extensive renovations Henry Clay Mill was reopened in the 1950s as the information center for the Hagley Foundation. The museum contains a giant topographical map of the Brandywine River Valley and several exhibits that depict the early history of the du Pont family and the black powder industry.

After the Revolutionary War, Americans determined to produce for themselves the products they previously had imported. The availability of raw materials, the strong waterpower, good transportation, and proximity to markets made the Brandywine Valley an ideal site for milling operations.

The exhibits in Henry Clay Mill trace the history of American manufacturing along the Brandywine River. Excellent working models demonstrate early machinery and power sources. The models are made with exquisite attention to detail. The working model of Oliver Evans's automated flour mill is outstanding.

From Henry Clay Mill visitors may walk or take a three-mile jitney ride to enjoy the restored mills, working demonstrations, dams, millraces, and scenery along the Brandywine Creek. The jitney takes visitors to the first Delaware home of the du Pont family and the first office of the DuPont Company.

This view of Henry Clay Mill is probably seen by very few of the thousands of visitors to Hagley. I wanted to paint the mill but needed an interesting foreground. In my search for an appropriate spot I happened on the mill race gate. I had been to Hagley countless times but had never ventured into this out-of-the-way and rather secluded spot.

36" x 24" Oil on canvas 1992 Corporate Collection

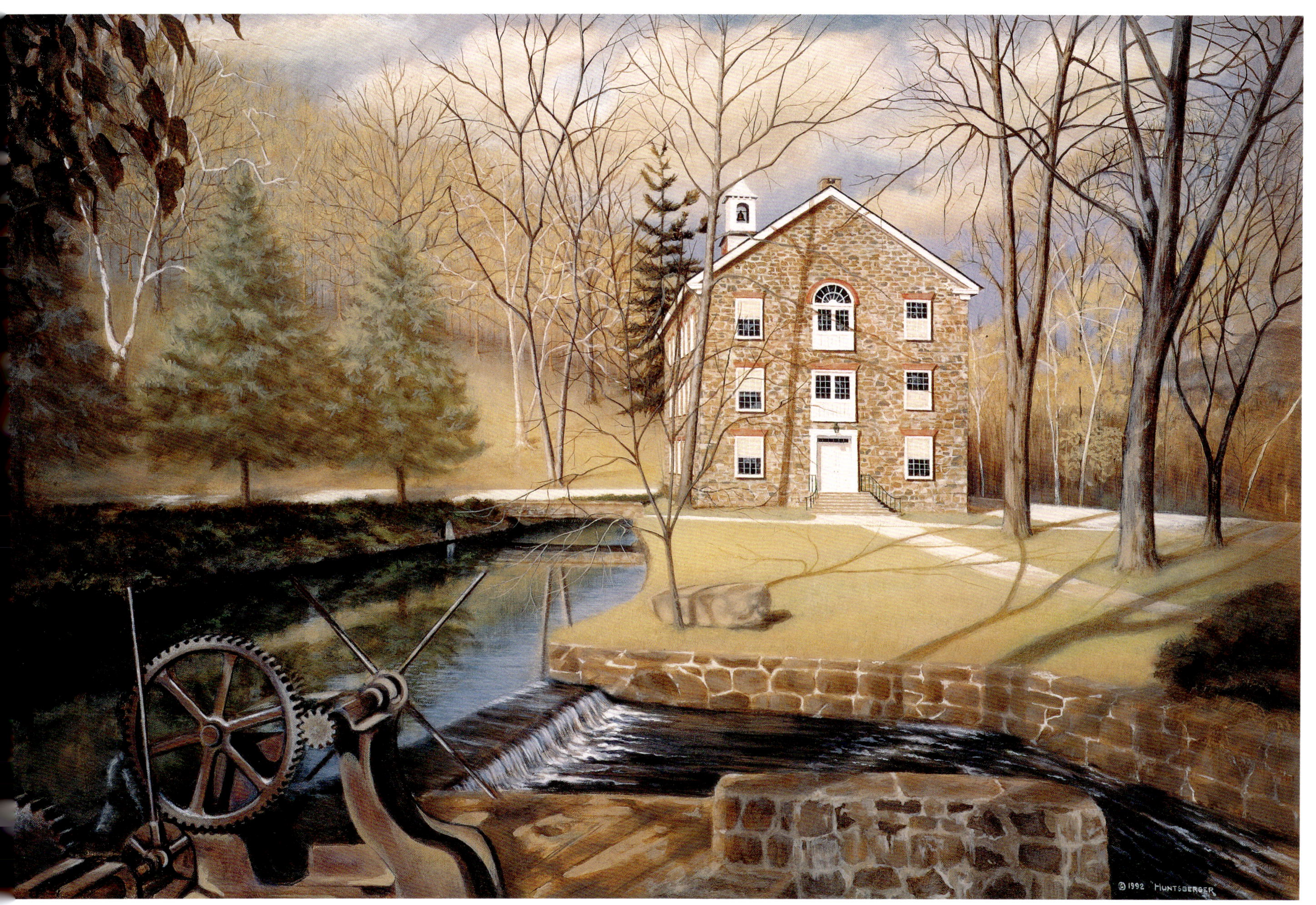
© 1992 "HUNTSBERGER"

The Powder Mill

After discovering the poor quality of American gunpowder, E. I. du Pont decided to manufacture black powder. Because he had studied under Lavoisier, he knew he could make a superior product.

Powder was made by combining and grinding charcoal, saltpeter, and sulfur under large iron wheels in rolling mills, followed by pressing to remove water and drying in the sun. After sizing, polishing, and sifting to remove dust, it was packed into wooden kegs.

When I moved to Wilmington in 1958, I found the grounds at Hagley a wonderful place to explore with my young son. This was prior to the extensive restoration. I found the remains of the mills fascinating. They remain so to me today, and I have enjoyed painting several of them.

24" x 18" Oil on canvas 1995

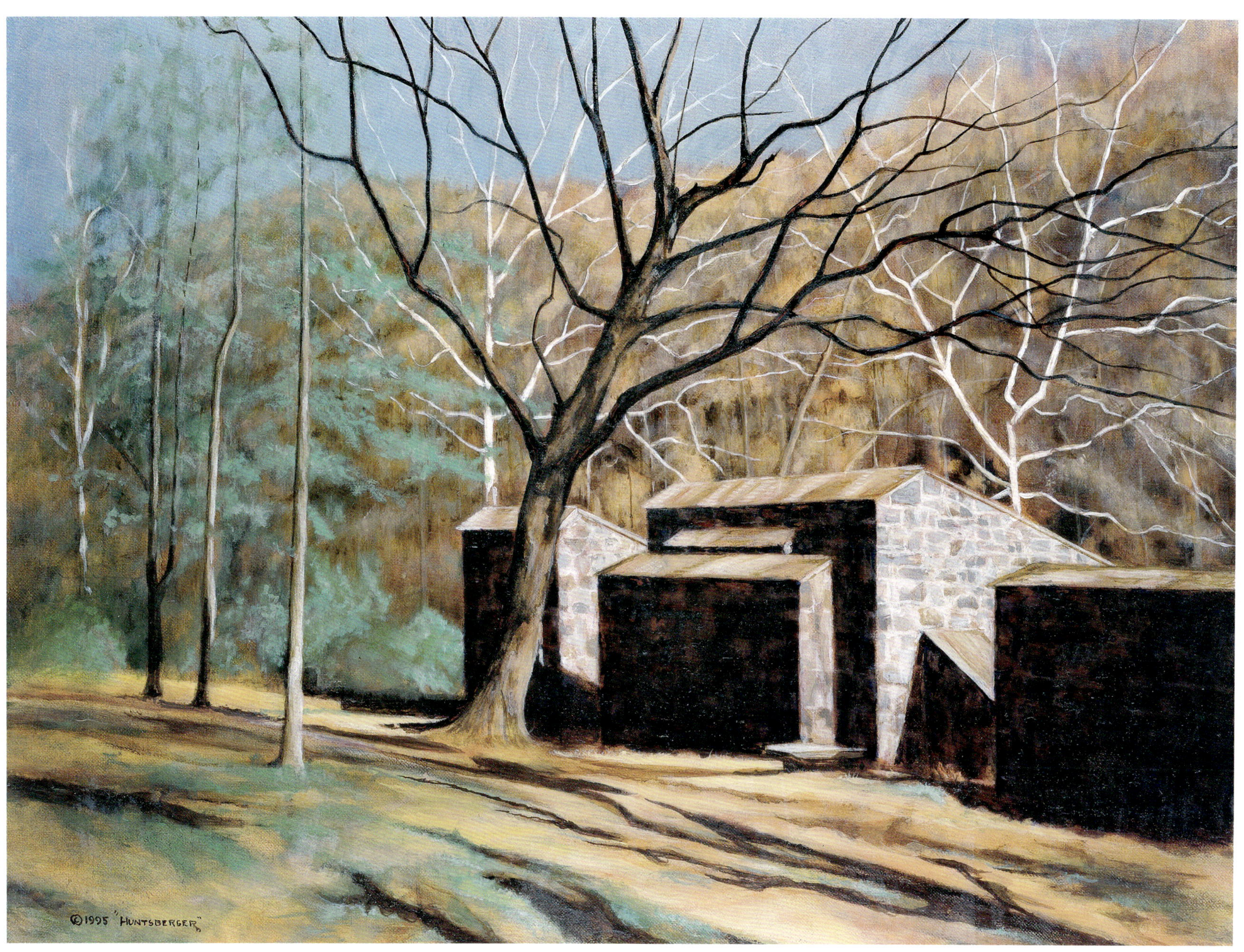
©1995 "HUNTSBERGER"

The Birkenhead Powder Mill

(The Mill)

This painting is of one of the pair of Birkenhead Powder Mills built in 1822-1824 between the Brandywine Creek and the millrace. The DuPont Company built rolling mills in pairs with large wooden water wheels between them to provide power.

For greatest safety the three-foot-thick stone building had a wooden wall on the riverside, topped by a breakaway roof designed to blow out over the river in the event of an explosion, protecting workers from the blast.

Shortly after World War I the powder yards were abandoned and the mills fell into disrepair. The Birkenhead Mills became overgrown with trees, and the water wheel collapsed.

Today Birkenhead has been completely restored—water wheel and all. The dead tree that I found so attractive in the 1960s has been removed, so my painting is just a glimpse of a world that no longer exists.

30" x 24" Oil on canvas 1996 Private Collection

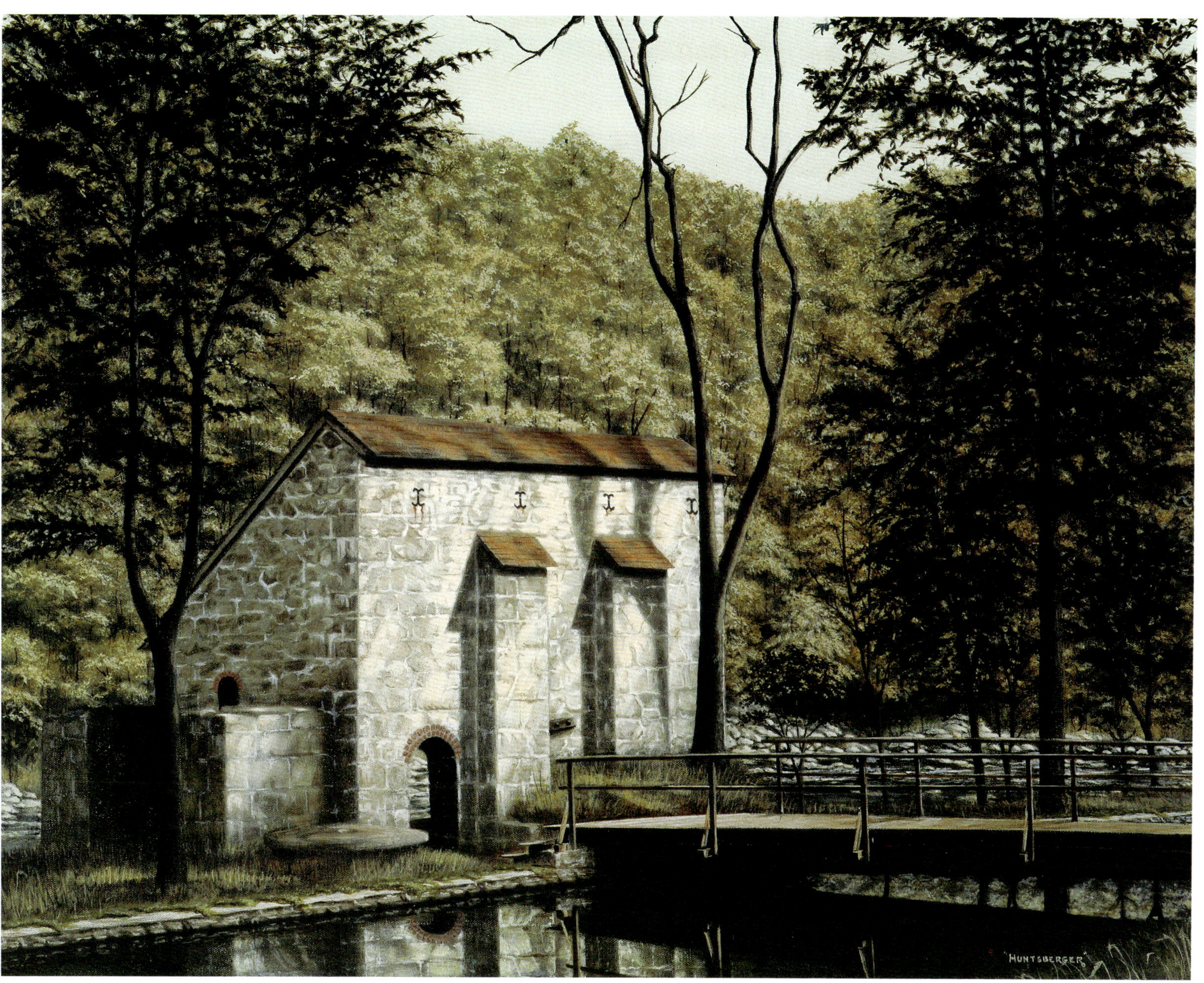
"HUNTSBERGER"

Graining Mill

This graining mill is one of the many DuPont mills built along Brandywine Creek between 1802 and 1850 to produce black powder. Like the Birkenhead Mill, this graining mill has three-foot-thick walls on three sides, a lightweight wooden wall toward the river, and a breakaway roof slanted toward the river to reduce damage in case of lightning strike or accident.

Powder was produced here for every important battle in the War of 1812. Union troops guarded the Hagley Yards during the Civil War. Little powder was produced during World War I, and all powder production ceased at Hagley in 1921.

This painting was an experiment in color. I thought it would be fun to go a bit wild to see what the result might be. Others also enjoyed the results, for the painting was accepted in a Wayne (Pennsylvania) Art Center National Juried Art Show in 1999.

20” x 16” Oil on canvas 1998

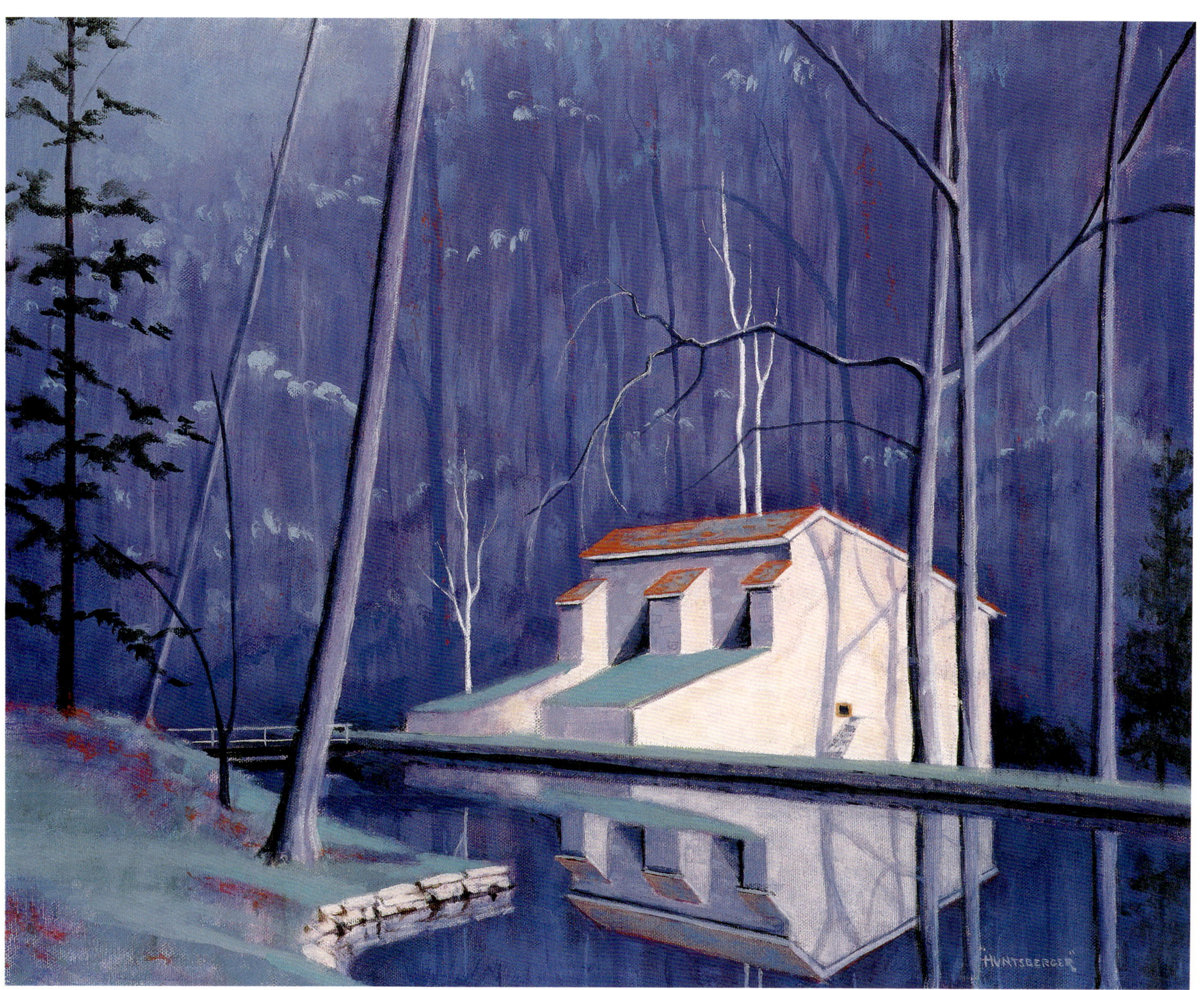
HUNTSBERGER

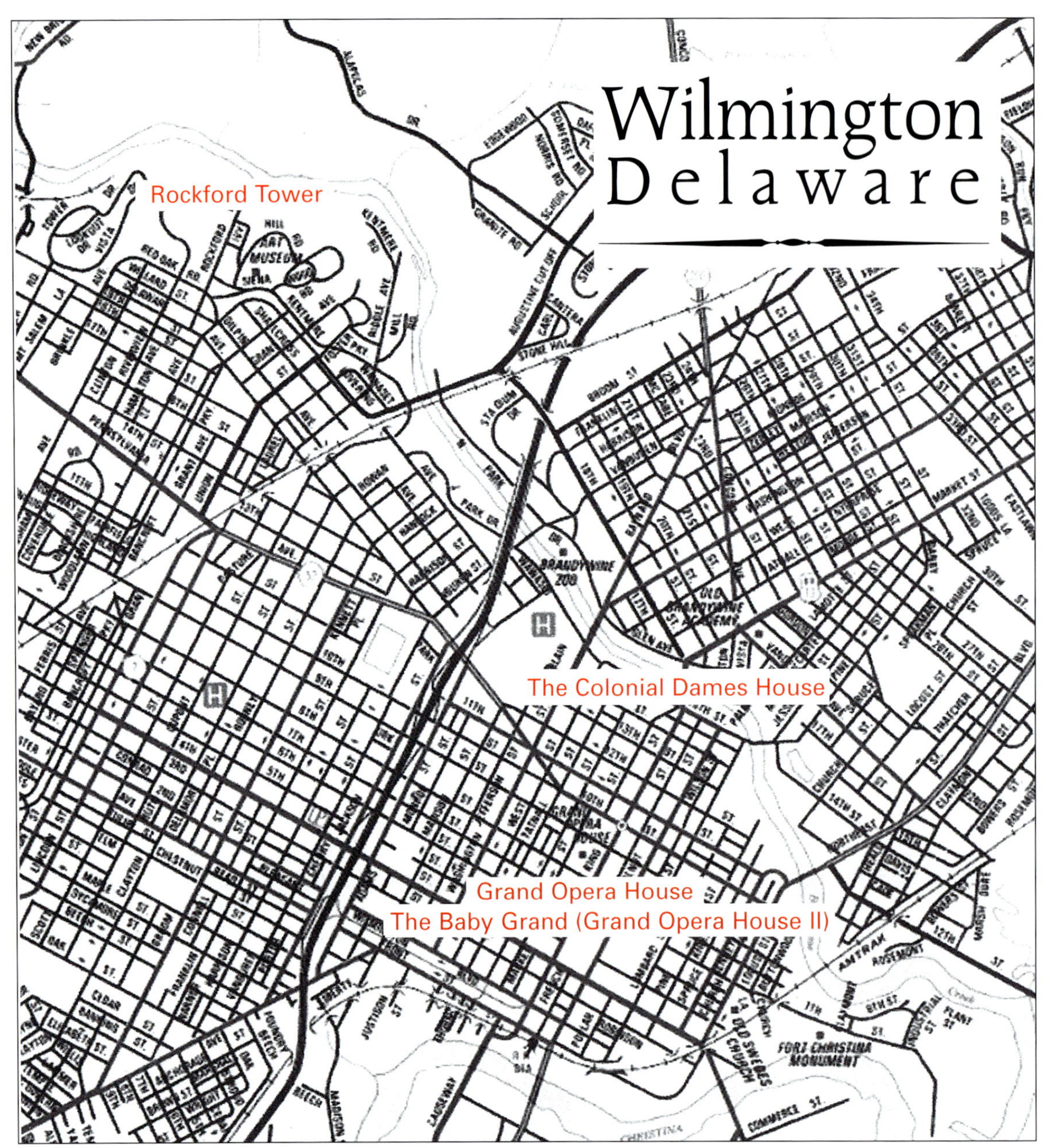
Wilmington
Delaware
Rockford Tower
The Colonial Dames House
Grand Opera House
The Baby Grand (Grand Opera House II)

CHAPTER SEVEN

Wilmington, Delaware

In 1638 Peter Minuit of the Swedish Trading Company and twenty-four settlers from Sweden, Finland, Holland, and Germany landed on Christiana Creek. A replica of their ship, Kalmar Nyckel, has been created. The ship represents Delaware at tall ships festivals from Massachusetts to Virginia.

Following the early settlers were additional Swedish, Dutch, and English immigrants. Contention for control of the land existed among these groups until William Penn arrived in 1682 to establish English rule.

In 1731 Thomas Willing mapped out the site of modern-day Wilmington, which was originally called Willington. The name was later changed to honor Lord Wilmington.

Flour milling was the first industry in Wilmington. By 1764 eight mills had been established on the Brandywine. Wilmington's many chemical industries began when the du Pont family started making black powder in 1803. Several major chemical firms are located in Wilmington.

Wilmington has been called the chemical capital of the world because of its concentration of major chemical companies. When I arrived in Wilmington in 1958, DuPont, Hercules, and Atlas were the major ones along with several minor ones. Atlas has undergone a succession of owners and is currently Astra Zeneca.

Rockford Tower

Rockford Tower is the centerpiece of Rockford Park, located on land donated by William P. Bancroft. Built of native stone and topped with a tile roof, the 115-foot-tall tower contains a 500,000-gallon tank, which is part of Wilmington's water supply. A large sun dial graces the south façade. A 199-step spiral stairway leads to an observation platform seventy-five feet above the ground. The tower's inner walls are glazed white to reflect light that enters through narrow slit windows.

Fifteen archways circle the platform to provide panoramic views and frame these favorite Brandywine Valley landmarks: Tower Hill School, the city of Wilmington, the Delaware River with New Jersey beyond, the wooded regions of the Brandywine Hills and the A. I. du Pont Memorial Carillon Tower, the DuPont Experimental Station with the DuPont Country Club, and Henry Clay Village with large estates beyond.

Closed for renovations for many years, the tower reopened to visitors in 2002.

Rockford Tower is to Wilmington what the Charles Bridge is to Prague, the Chain Bridge to Budapest, or the Eiffel Tower to Paris. It has been the subject of paintings by many artists; consequently, I had not considered it as one I should attempt. However, when I was in Rockford Park in autumn, this view with the vibrant fall foliage persuaded me to join the crowd.

20" x 16" Oil on canvas 1997 Corporate Collection

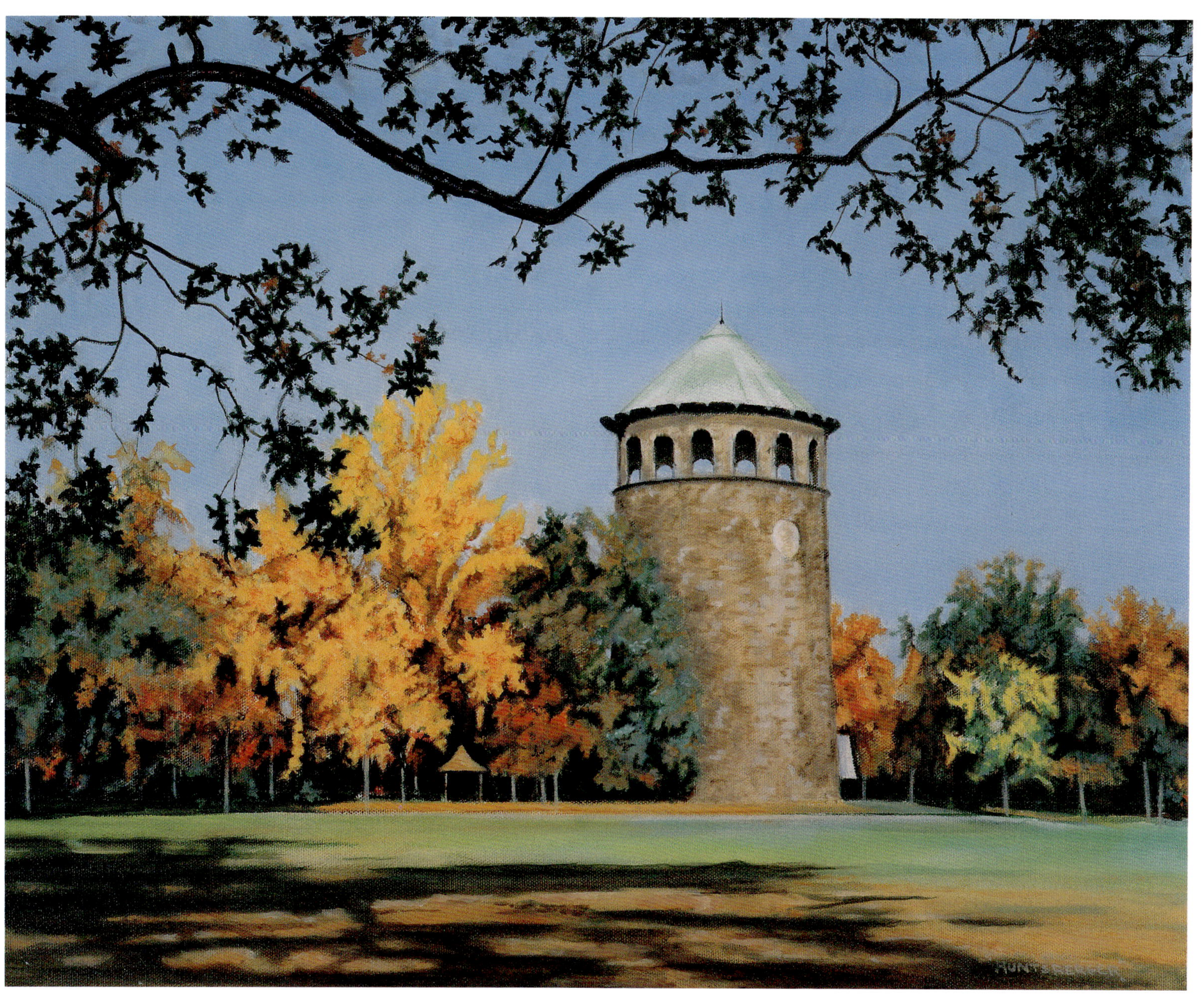

Grand Opera House

In 1871 the Delaware Lodge of Ancient Free and Accepted Masons built its Masonic Temple on the east side of Market Street south of Ninth Street. The major portion of the building contained the Grand Opera House, a theatre seating fourteen hundred people. Its large, well-equipped stage attracted the best musical and theatrical productions of the time.

The Grand Opera House opened on Christmas Day 1871 with Daisy Farm as the matinee and Rob Roy in the evening. Numerous operatic groups and many noted actors, including Edwin Booth, George M. Cohan, and Ethel Barrymore, appeared there.

Over the years this grand building became shabby and, during the mid-twentieth century, degenerated into a second-rate movie theater.

Completely renovated during the 1970s, the Grand Opera House presents the finest in performing arts, in addition to the local talent of the Delaware Symphony and OperaDelaware.

The façade of this grand old structure is quite charming. Finding a viewpoint that included what I wished to paint was difficult. It required many visits to the scene plus a bit of imagination to paint this. There is no single place to see what I have developed for this painting.

24" x 18" Oil on canvas 1995 Corporate Collection

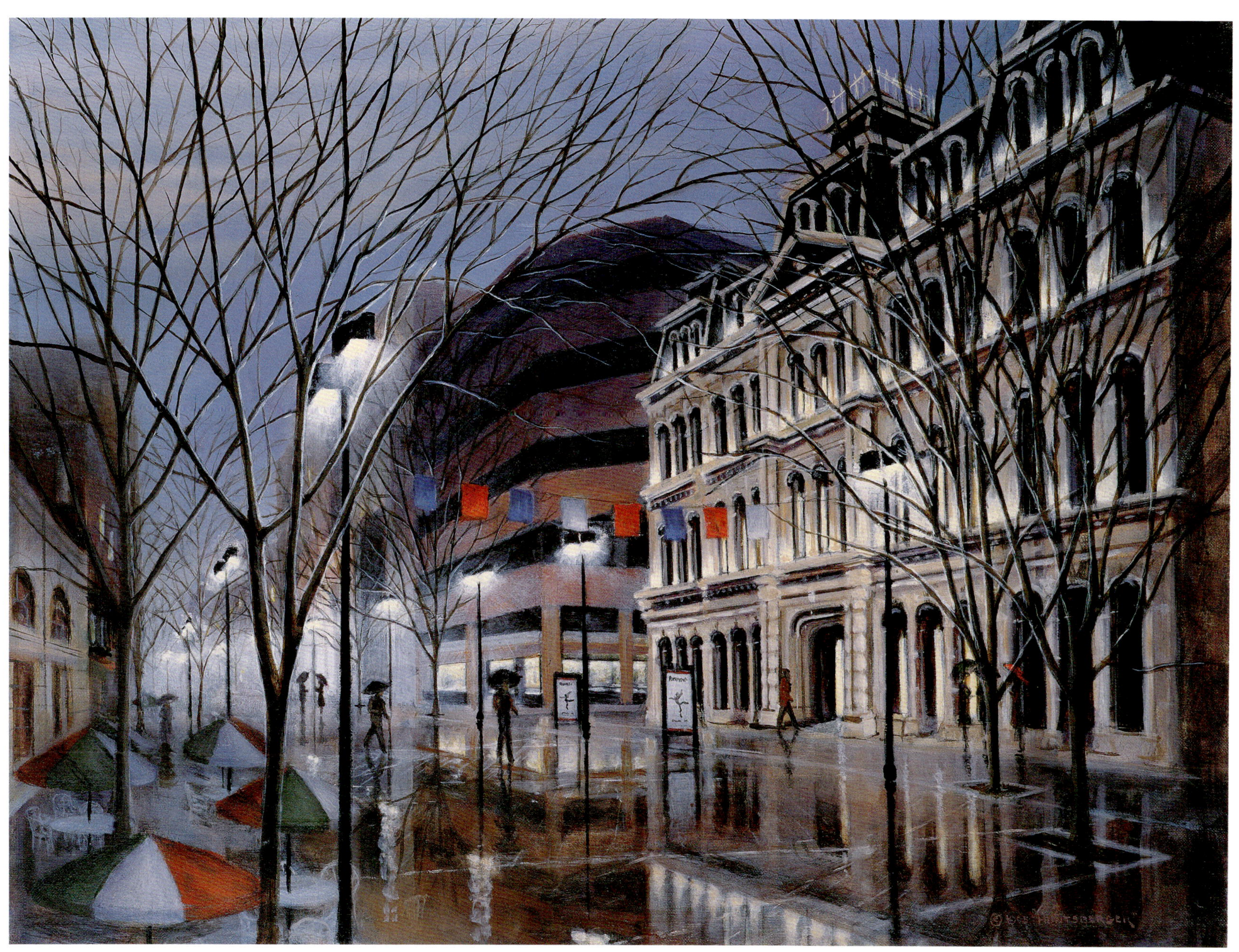

The Baby Grand

Kenneth Wesler, executive director of the Grand Opera House, spearheaded the renovation of an old store adjoining the opera house to form The Delaware Center for the Performing Arts. Completed in 2000, the center was named the Edith and Alexander Giacco building in honor of the former chairman of the Grand Opera House and his late wife.

The centerpiece of this renovation is a three-hundred-seat theater called "The Baby Grand." The small space provides an intimate setting for performances. The center also houses six dressing rooms, 17,000 square feet of rehearsal and studio space, an art gallery, and administrative offices for the Grand Opera House, Delaware Symphony Orchestra, and OperaDelaware.

This painting was reproduced as the program booklet cover for all arts programming for the 2001-2004 Grand Opera House seasons.

24" x 18" Oil on canvas 2001 Collection of Kenneth & Deborah Wesler

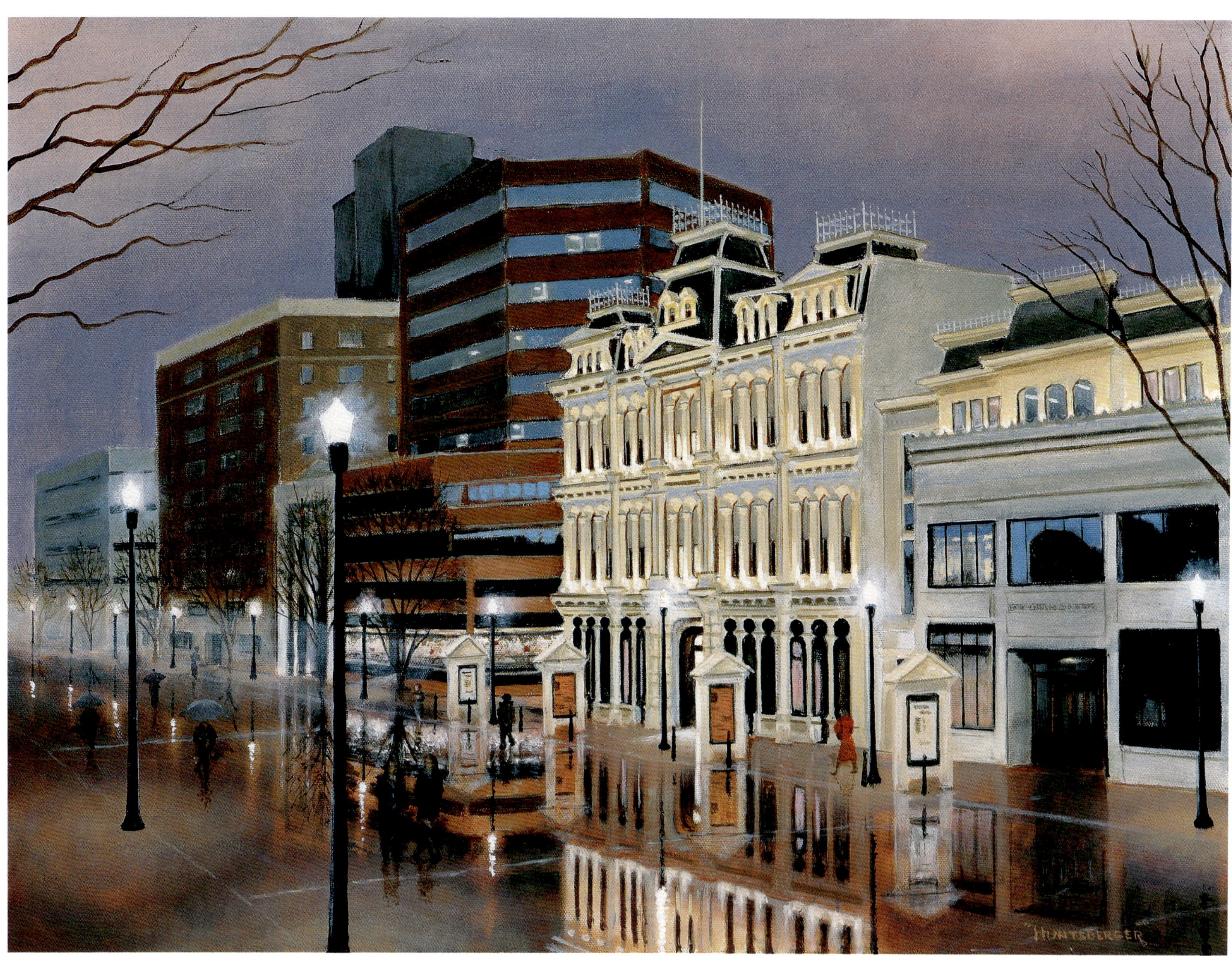
HUNTSBERGER

The Colonial Dames House

This small Dutch Colonial red brick building was built on the east side of Market Street in 1740 as the First Presbyterian Meeting House of Wilmington, Delaware. The gambrel-roofed building's panel doors have an arched fanlight that echoes the design of the arched, white-shuttered windows.

When British troops occupied Wilmington on September 12, 1777, after the Battle of Brandywine, they used the church as a prison or hospital. In 1840 a new church was built, and this meeting house was remodeled as a Sunday school.

In 1916 the Market Street property was chosen for the site of the Wilmington Public Library; thus the Sunday school was slated for demolition. Fortunately its present owners, the Colonial Dames of America, rescued the historical building and moved it to its present location on Park Drive and West Street on the west bank of Brandywine Creek.

The wonderful autumn colors coupled with the sweep of the road along the Brandywine made this scene an attractive setting for the splendid architecture of the Colonial Dames House.

20" x 16" Oil on canvas 2001 Collection of Mrs. David Craven

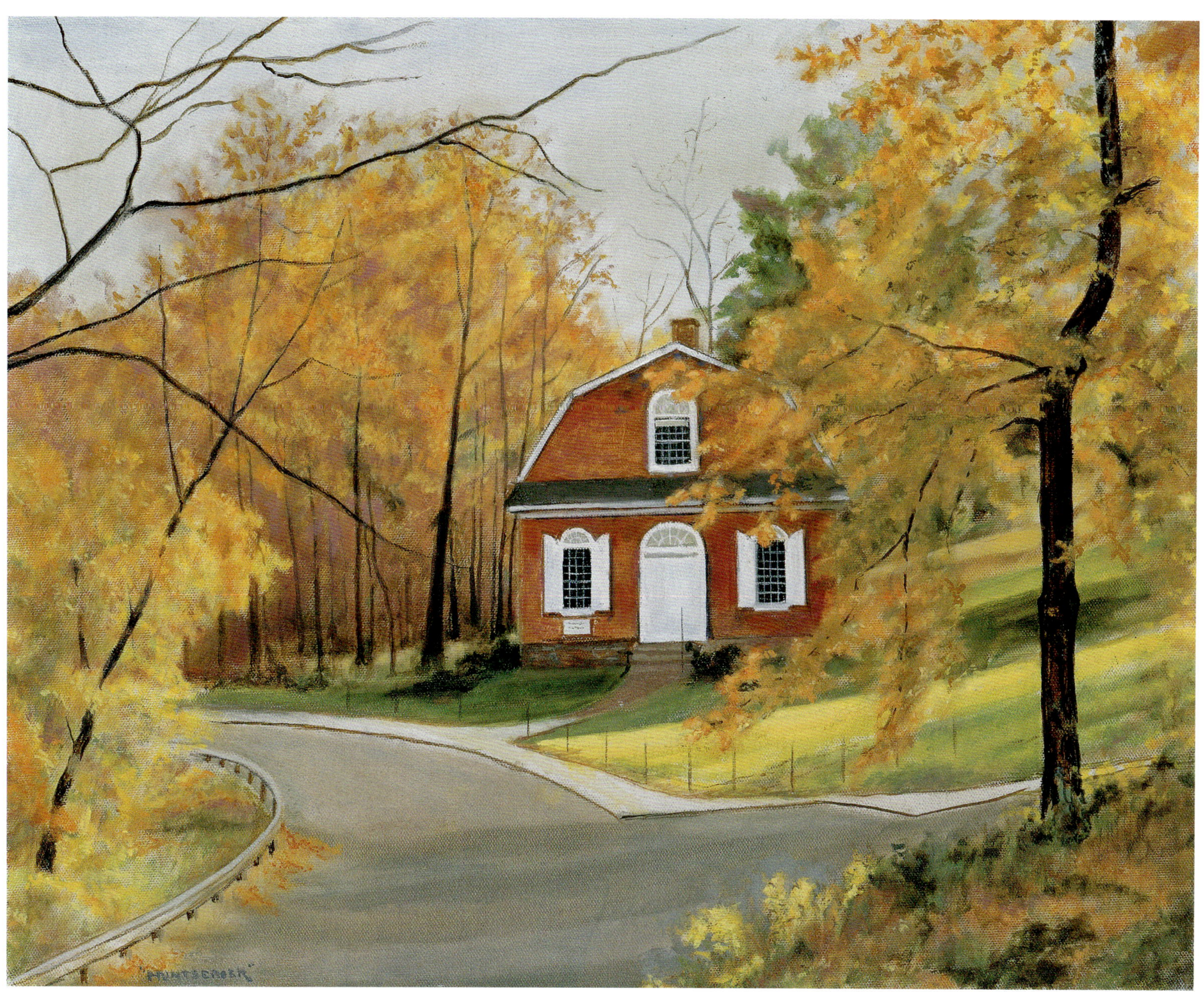

Chapter Eight

Close to Home

Red Maple

I know this tree very well because I planted it in 1966. It is just beyond our patio and frames the view of our back lawn. It is now about thirty-five-feet tall. During the autumn, when viewed with translucent light, the leaves are brilliant. I thought this would make a rather striking painting. It certainly did invite attention and comment when we displayed it.

36" x 36" Oil on canvas 1992 Corporate Collection

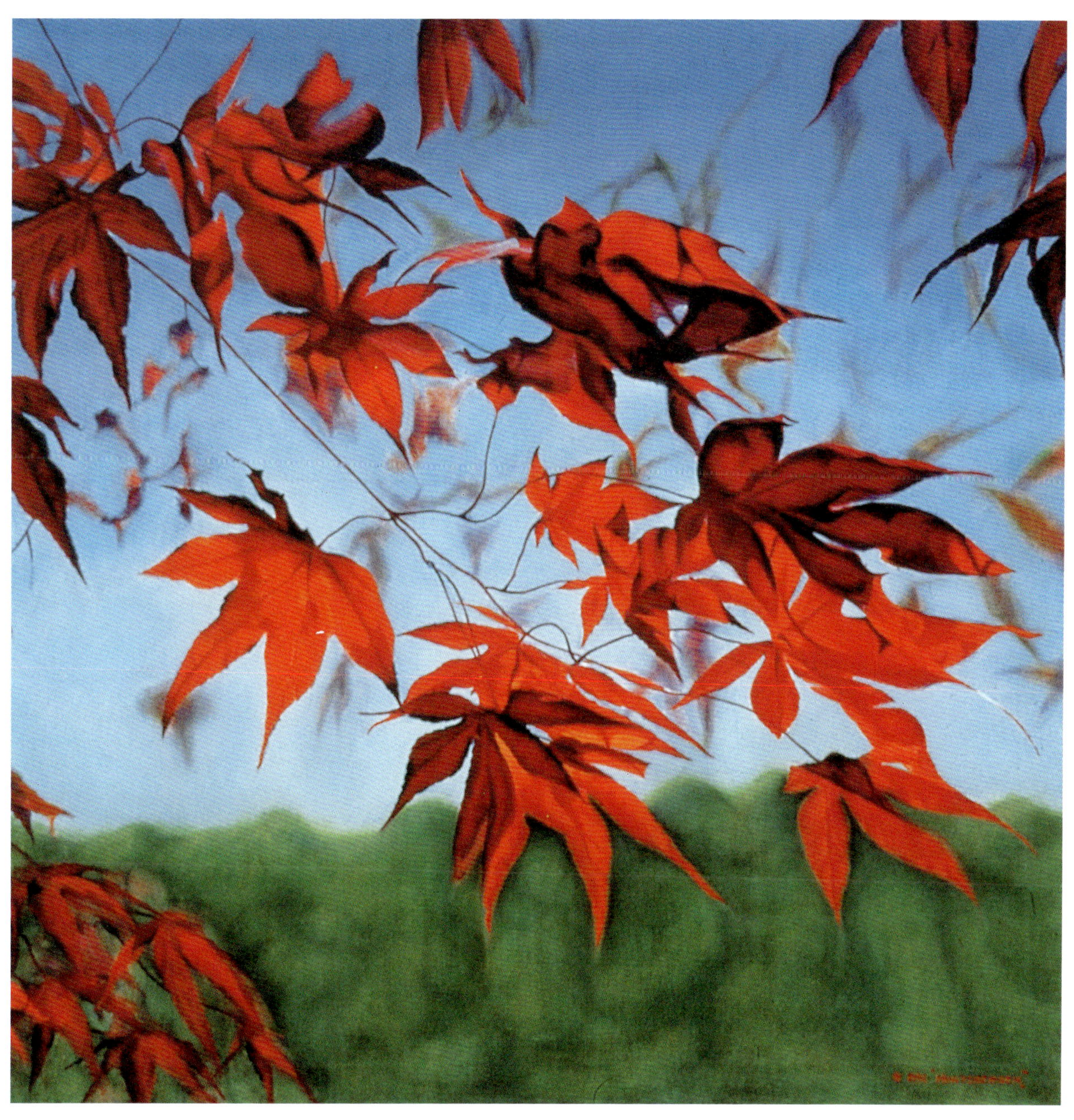

Sunset III

The endless variety of patterns and colors provided by skies, clouds, and sunsets are among nature's most lovely displays. I have enjoyed painting the somber sky depicted in End of an Era, the brilliant skies of Mallard Pond and September, and many sunsets. This is one viewed from my studio.

36" x 36" Oil on canvas 1991 Corporate Collection

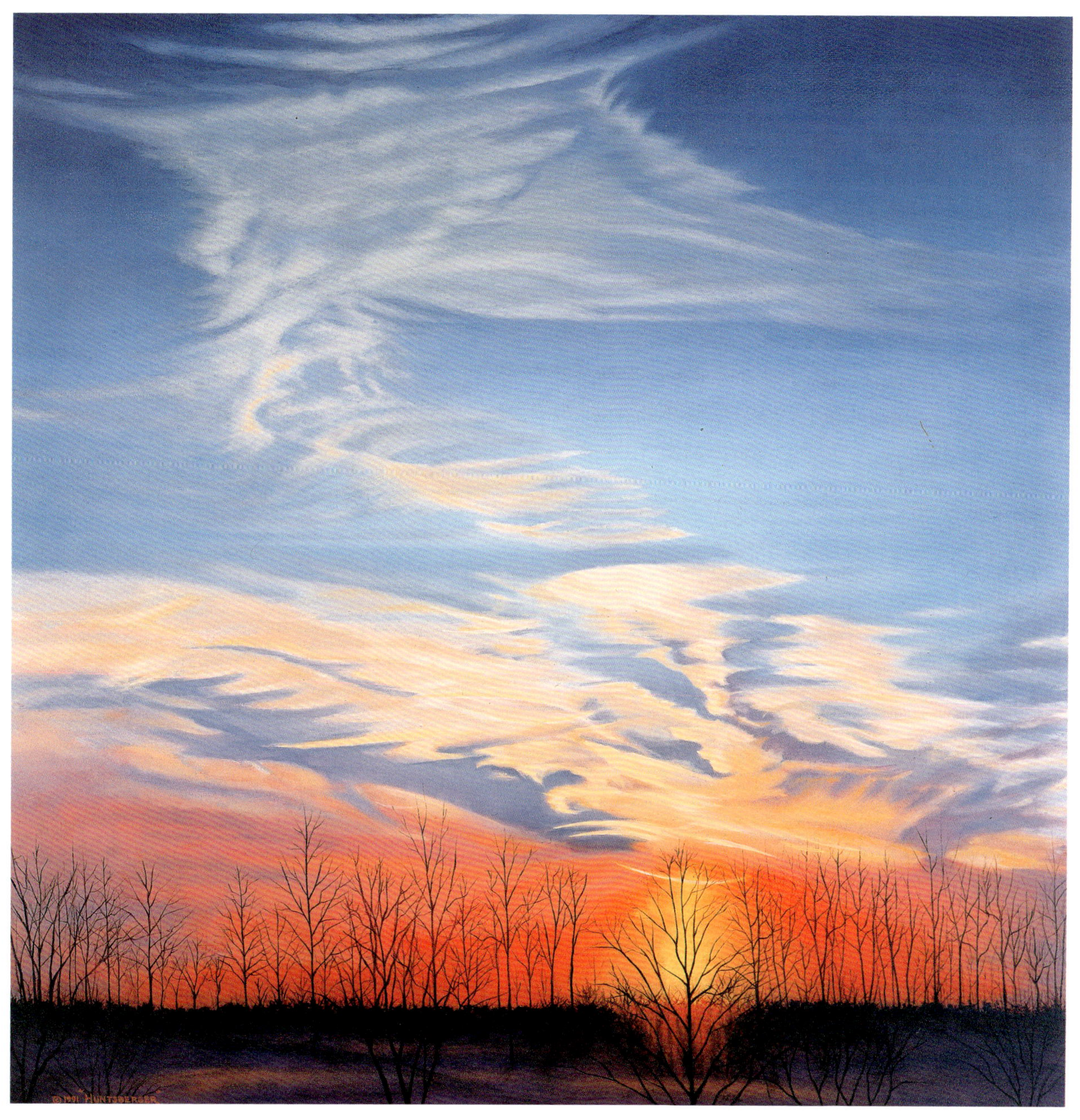
© 1991 HUNTSBERGER

Yellow Rhododendron

This yellow rhododendron is a treasured specimen on our property. It was so small when we planted it that we had trouble finding it in the surrounding pachysandra. Now it is four feet tall and produces a dozen huge blossoms each spring.

20” x 24” Oil on canvas 2002 Collection of Mr. and Mrs. Brian Dalphon

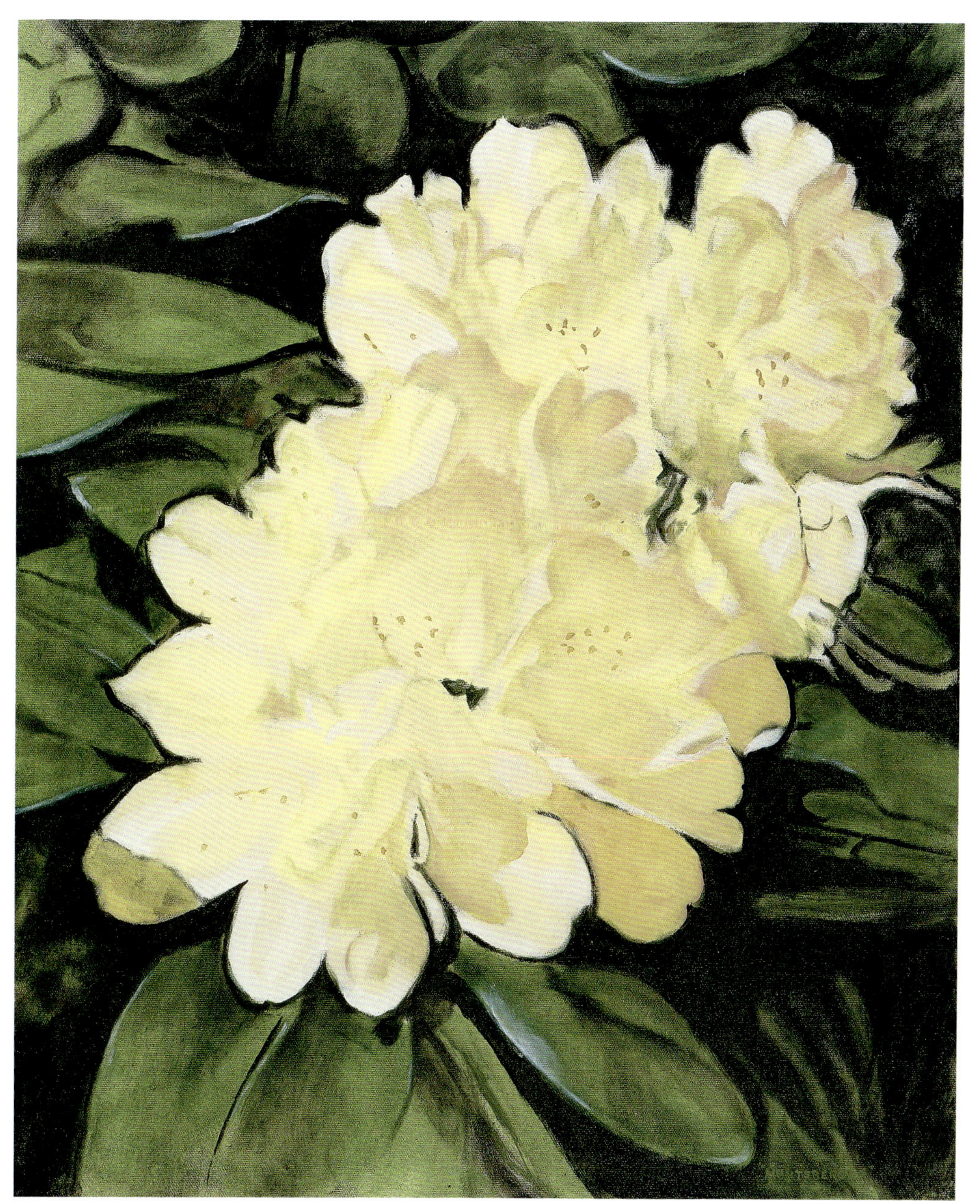

Amaryllis

Each autumn Janet plants amaryllis bulbs to produce flowers to enjoy when the garden is covered with snow. During January 2003 this dwarf amaryllis with the huge white blossoms sat on our dining room windowsill. This is the loveliest amaryllis we have grown.

16” x 20” Oil on canvas 2003 Collection of Mrs. David Craven

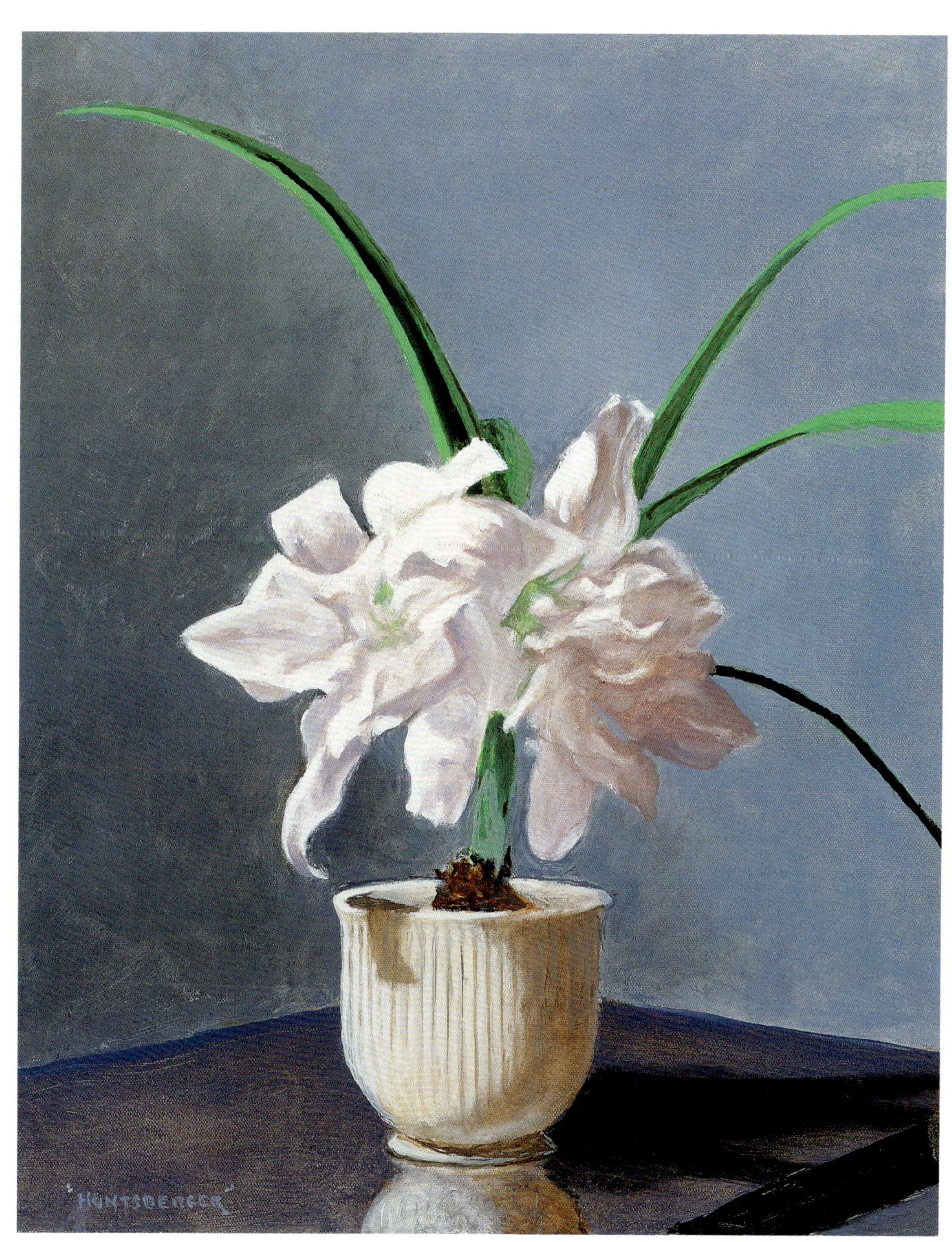
HUNTSBERGER

ANNOTATED BIBLIOGRAPHY

Suggestions for further reading and web sites to visit.

Canby, Henry Seidel. *The Brandywine.* 1941.
Exton, Pennsylvania., Schiffer Ltd.
Mr. Canby tells the history of the Brandywine River as it flows from Southeastern Pennsylvania into the Christiana River in Wilmington, Delaware. This five-by-eight-inch volume is illustrated by twenty-two black-and-white drawings by Andrew Wyeth, who at age twenty-four was beginning his distinguished career. He has become one of America's best-known artists. The author is descended from families that have lived in the region for generations. Mr. Canby's charming and well-written history belongs in the library of anyone interested in the Brandywine Valley. The Brandywine is a classic book, which will continue to receive attention through the years because it is informative and well written.

Dell, John Edward, Editor. *Visions of Adventure: N. C. Wyeth and the Brandywine Artists.* 2000.
New York, Watson-Guptill Publications.
This book profiles six artists: N.C. Wyeth, Howard Pyle, Harvey Dunn, Frank Schoonover, Philip R. Goodwin, and Dean Cornwell. This handsome volume contains many reproductions of the illustrations these artists painted for popular books and magazines during the twentieth century. A beautifully illustrated book about the artists and their art, this book has little information about the Brandywine Valley area and no paintings of local scenes. If one is interested in artists of the Brandywine School, this book will be of special interest.

Matuszewski, Barbara Bell. *Bounty on the Brandywine: A Heritage of Natural Beauty, History, Art and Fine Food.* 1988.
Wilmington, Delaware, The Middle Atlantic Press.
This attractive six-by-nine-inch book is an expanded recipe book. Its first fifty pages are devoted to the history, art history, descriptions of the Brandywine Valley, and a gazetteer containing brief descriptions of local highlights. The next 267 pages are devoted to recipes. Full-color reproductions of paintings owned by the author or her parents mark the beginning of each chapter.

Monty, Lise. Photographs by Mike Biggs. *Images of Delaware.* 1998.
Wilmington, Delaware, Miller Publishing, Inc.
With its forward by John M. Burris, former president of the Delaware Chamber of Commerce, this appears to be a completely updated version of a fifty-year-old book, which was produced to encourage businesses to settle in Delaware. Images of Delaware has informative, well-written text, photographs of Delaware, and a chapter about each of the several corporations that sponsored its publication.

Pitz, Henry C. *The Brandywine Tradition.* 1968.
Boston, Houghton Mifflin Company.
This book is illustrated by sixteen color plates and thirty-two black-and-white plates of Brandywine School art, bound in distinct sections rather than distributed throughout the seven-by-ten-inch text. It features a brief history of the Brandywine Valley, the Battle of Brandywine, a comprehensive biography of Howard Pyle, and a history of Pyle's influence on Brandywine Valley art.

Pitz covers Pyle's teaching at Drexel Institute of Art in Philadelphia and his own schools in Chadds Ford and Wilmington. This is an excellent volume if one is particularly interested in Brandywine Valley art.

Wamsley, James S. Photographs by Steven Mays. *The Brandywine Valley: An Introduction to its Cultural Treasures.* 1992.
New York, Harry N. Abrams, Inc., Publishers.
This handsome nine-by-twelve-inch book details the nine major local museums. They are the Historical Society of Delaware, the Hagley Museum, Rockwood, Winterthur, the Delaware Art Museum, Nemours, the Delaware Museum of Natural History, the Brandywine River Museum, and Longwood Gardens.
This is the definitive volume about these museums (as they were in 1992) because the information was gathered and edited with the help of the public relations departments of the institutions.
Mr. Mays's photographs complement old pictures from the archives. Changes have been made in almost all of these institutions since 1992, so this book will not substitute for a visit now. It will, however, give one an excellent introduction to major cultural landmarks in the Brandywine Valley.

Westerman, Carla. *Chadds Ford: History, Heroes and Landmarks.* 2003.
Gettysburg, Pennsylvania, Thomas Publications.
Carla Westerman has produced a handsome guidebook and keepsake of Chadds Ford, Pennsylvania. This slim volume is packed with Westerman's excellent photographs and well-written commentary and history of the little village that forms the heart of the Brandywine Valley. Westerman's background as a writer for The Kennett Paper covering Chadds Ford stories and her interest in eighteenth-century American history have combined to make this a useful book for visitors and residents alike.

Zeidner, Lisa. Photographs by Anthony Edgeworth. *Brandywine: A Legacy of Tradition in du Pont-Wyeth Country.* 1995.
Charlottesville, Virginia, Thomasson-Grant Publishers.
This is a nine-by-twelve-inch volume of excellent photographs accompanied by text. Six topics are covered: 1) An Introduction gives a brief history of the Brandywine Valley, 2) Delaware Dynasty is an overview of the du Pont family, 3) Gardens and Houses tells about the Longwood and Mt. Cuba gardens, as well as the gardens and houses at Nemours and Winterthur, 4) Horses and Dogs is mainly photographs of local fox hunting tradition, 5) The Land tells of forming the Brandywine Conservancy to protect the land from industrial development, 6) The Art has information about the Delaware Art Museum and Brandywine River Museum, three local sculptors, and Andrew and James Wyeth. An excellent photographer, Mr. Edgeworth had access to individuals and places most people will never see and gives us an upscale "insiders" view of the Brandywine Valley.

Web sites

www.brandywinevalley.com—tourist information.

www.thebrandywine.com—lists area attractions.

www.hsd.org—the Historical Society of Delaware.

www.wilmcvb.org—Wilmington Convention Bureau.

www.chaddsfordhistory.org—Chadds Ford Historical Society.

SOURCES

Bibliography

Bathe, Greville and Dorothy Bathe. *Oliver Evans: A Chronicle of Early American Engineering.*
Philadelphia, Pennsylvania: Historical Society of Pennsylvania, 1935.

Beach, John W. *Cape Henlopen Lighthouse and Delaware Breakwater.*
Dover, Delaware: Dover Graphics Assoc., 1980.

Cantor, Jay E. *Winterthur.*
New York: Harry N. Abrams, Inc., 1985.

Detchon, Helen A. and Elliott R. *The "Go....Don't Go" Guide to Delaware and Nearby Pennsylvania.*
Helen A. and Elliott R. Detchon, 1976.

Eckman, Jeannette. *Delaware: A Guide to the First State.*
New York: Hastings House, 1976.

Harrison, Marina and Lucy D. Rosenfeld. *Gardenwalks.*
New York: Michael Kesend Publishing, 1997.

Lord, Ruth. *Henry F. du Pont and Winterthur, A Daughter's Portrait.*
New Haven, Conneticut, and London, England: Yale University Press, 1999.

MacDonald, Betty Harrington. *Historical Landmarks of Delaware and the Eastern Shore*.
Wilmington, Deaware.: Delaware State Society of the Daughters of the American Colonists, 1976.

McNinch, Marjorie G. *Bridges.*
Wilmington, Delaware: The Cedar Tree Press, Inc., 1995.

PAC Spero and Company of Baltimore, Maryland. *Delaware Historical Bridges Survey and Evaluation.*
Dover, Delaware: Delaware Dept. of Transportation, 1991.

Schiffer, Margaret Benwind. *Survey of Chester County Pennsylvania Architecture: 17th, 18th and 19th Centuries.*
Exton, Pennsylvania: Schiffer Publishing Ltd., 1976.

Taber, William S. *Delaware Trees.*
Dover, Delaware: Delaware State Forestry Dept., 1937.

Twaddell, Meg Daley. *Inns, Tales and Taverns of Chester County.*
Country Publications, Inc., 1984.

Other Sources

The Battle of Brandywine: 11 September 1777. Translated by Bruce E. Burgoyne.

Blume, Cara Lee, et al. *Brandywine State Creek Park.* A report submitted to the Delaware Division of Historical and Cultural Affairs, 1990.

Brosch, Florence Betts Cloud. *Chadds Ford as I Remember It.* Library of the Chadds Ford Historical Society.

The Book of the State of Delaware. As set forth by the command of the governor and his commissioners to the Jamestown Exposition of 1901.

Hoke, Donald S. An Echo on the Brandywine. Pocopson, Pennsylvania: Echo.

Milton, John. *Bringing History Back to Life.* Chadds Ford, Pennsylvania: Chadds Ford Historical Society.

The Hunt. Wilmington, Delaware: Today Media, Inc., Holiday, 2001.

Reed, John F. *Campaign to Valley Forge: July 1, 1777 to December 19, 1777.* Philadelphia, Pennsylvania: Pioneer Press, The Trustees of the University of Pennsylvania, 1965.

Toro, Lucille P. *The Latrobe Survey of New Castle, Delaware in 1804-1805*. Newark, Delaware: University of Delaware, Thesis as requirement for a degree of master of arts in history, 1971.

Web sites

www.brandywinemuseum.org

www.brandywineconservancy.org

www.geography.about.com/library/weekly

www.grandopera.org

www.hagley.lib.de.us/museum.html

www.longwoodgardens.org

www.udel.edu

www.winterthur.org

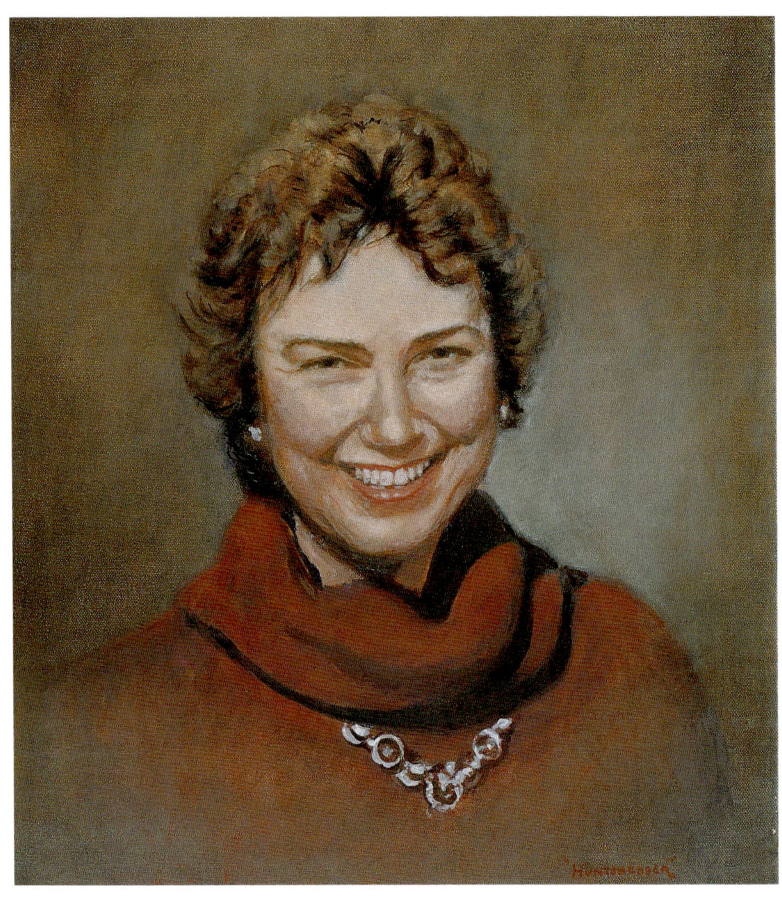

16" x 20" Oil on Canvas 2003
Collection of Janet and James Huntsberger

Janet Davis Huntsberger

Janet Davis Huntsberger, born in Des Moines, Iowa, is a descendant of Abigail Kimball and John Edmund Severance, who arrived in Massachusetts from England on the ship *Elizabeth* in 1634. She earned her bachelor and master of arts degrees at the University of Cincinnati where she was elected to Phi Beta Kappa.

During the 1970s, as director of alumni services at the University of Cincinnati, she initiated and directed two award-winning alumni programs: Alumni College (an informal education program for alumni taught by university faculty volunteers) and the Career Resource Center (a formal program to match University of Cincinnati students with alumni mentors). The Career Resource Center was funded by a grant from the W. K. Kellogg Foundation.

In 1982 Janet became the executive director of the Bryn Mawr College Alumnae Association. After her move to Delaware in 1985, she served as volunteer coordinator at the Delaware Museum of Natural History until she retired in 1993.

An admirer of her husband's paintings, Janet encouraged this volume. She maintains the website at www.art-hunt.com as part of managing practical aspects of showing and selling her husband's art.

James Robert Huntsberger (JR)

James Robert Huntsberger (JR), born in Harrisburg, Pennsylvania, is a descendant of one of three Swiss brothers who settled in that area before the Revolutionary War. He earned his bachelor of science degree at Bethany College and his Ph.D. at West Virginia University, where he trained as a chemist for his career as a research fellow with DuPont. During his years at DuPont his research focused on adhesion, rheology, surface chemistry, and the mechanical and optical properties of paint. He has lectured in the United States and abroad. His research writings have been published as journal articles and book chapters. He retired from DuPont in 1982.

JR has lived in Delaware since 1958. His career as a professional artist began in 1988 when he started selling his original oil paintings, which are now in private and corporate collections internationally.

All of his originals are oil paintings, and his subject matter includes portraits, seascapes, beach scenes, landscapes, still life, and historical structures. He has experimented with unusual subject matter and abstracted images but remains essentially a realist.

His oil paintings hang in Brandywine Valley galleries and are shown in more than twenty juried and charity art shows in the area each year. He has been the featured artist in several important regional charity art shows.

Selected to membership in The Philadelphia Sketch Club in 1991 and the Oil Painters of America in 1999, JR is a member of the Portrait Society of America, the Delaware Foundation for the Visual Arts, the Center for Creative Arts, the Chester County (Pennsylvania) Art Association, the Delaware Art Museum, the Brandywine Conservancy, the Delaware Center for the Contemporary Arts, the Woodmere Art Museum, and the Rehoboth Art League.

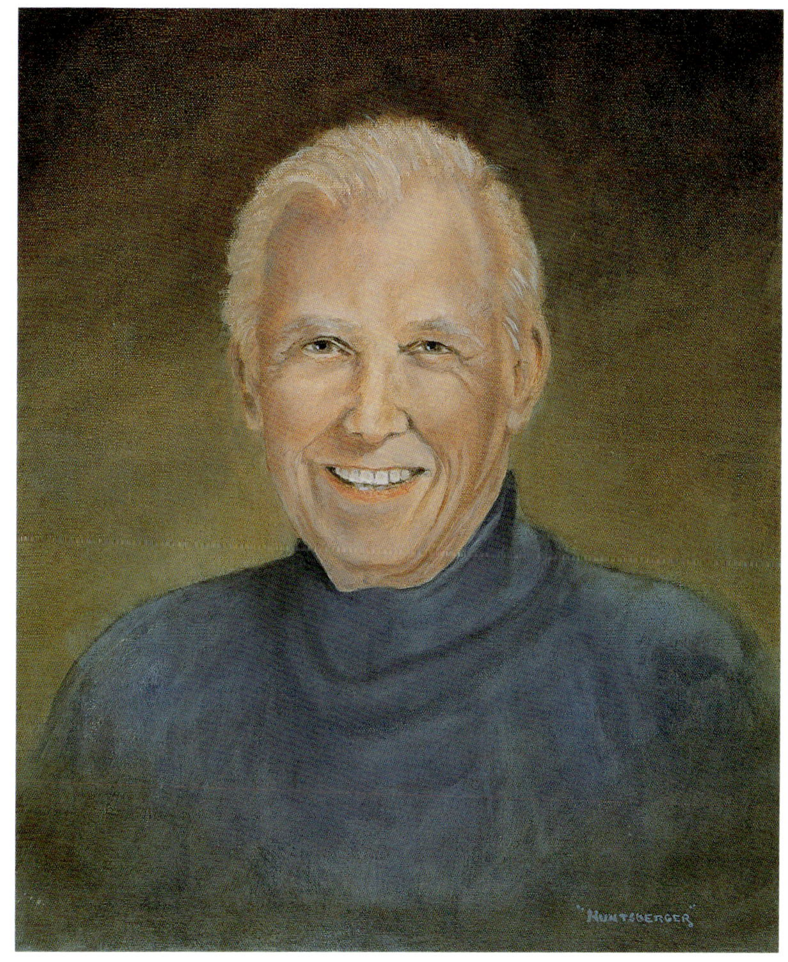

16" x 20" Oil on Canvas 2003
Collection of Janet and James Huntsberger

Index of Paintings